Nikitta

Nikitta

A MOTHER'S STORY

Marcia Grender
with Geraldine McKelvie

JOHN BLAKE

Published by John Blake Publishing Ltd,
3 Bramber Court, 2 Bramber Road,
London W14 9PB, England

www.johnblakebooks.com

www.facebook.com/johnblakebooks f
twitter.com/jblakebooks t

This edition published in 2016

ISBN: 978 1 78418 983 9

British Library Cataloguing-in-Publication Data:

A catalogue record for this book is available from the British Library.

Design by www.envydesign.co.uk

Printed in Great Britain by CPI Group (UK) Ltd

1 3 5 7 9 10 8 6 4 2

Papers used by John Blake Publishing are natural, recyclable products made
from wood grown in sustainable forests. The manufacturing processes
conform to the environmental regulations of the country of origin.

Every attempt has been made to contact the relevant copyright-holders,
but some were unobtainable. We would be grateful if the
appropriate people could contact us.

To our three girls: Nikitta, Kelsey-May and Missy

Contents

Prologue

*I*t's a hot summer's day – unusually hot for South Wales. I'm about ten, maybe eleven, and I'm running around my Nan's garden, playing with my cousins and feeling the hot sun on my forehead.

Although I remember this day so well, it's strange to think of me back in those days – a young and carefree child with no idea of the evil that exists in the world.

As I run through the long grass, I realise some of my cousins are tugging at my Nan's skirt, pleading with her to do something. I'm not sure what kind of plan they're hatching but I immediately decide I want in on it, so I run over to them.

'Please, Nan,' they are all saying. 'Please can you do it. Just this once?'

My Nan smiles softly, as if she's making up her mind. I'm still not sure what's going on, so I ask my cousins to explain.

'We want her to read our palms,' a little voice says. I'm not sure which one of my cousins it belongs to.

My Nan was descended from Romany gypsies and she always claimed she had some sort of sixth sense. As children, this fascinated us, naturally. As an adult, I'm much more sceptical but to this day it has always stuck in my mind.

'Oh, OK then,' she relents. 'Just this once.'

We sit in a circle at her feet and, one by one, she tells my cousins of their futures; of marriage and children and all sorts of other things that seem years off. I'm the last in the group and, by the time it becomes my turn, I'm already holding my hand out, expectantly.

My Nan takes it in hers but, as she does so, her smile fades and a strange expression flashes across her face. I know now what that emotion is: fear. Her leathery hands, which have turned brown in the sun, become unsteady. She tries and fails to smile as she pushes my hand away.

'Tell me, Nan!' I say. 'Tell me my future.'

She shakes her head. She's not smiling now; she's not even trying.

'No, Marce,' she says softly. 'When you're older.'

'But that's not fair!' I squeal. 'They all got to hear theirs!'

She is silent for a moment, before she nods solemnly and looks into my wide, childish eyes.

'I can't tell you now,' she says. 'I'll tell you when you're eighteen.' Her voice falters but only momentarily. 'If you really want to know,' she concludes.

In the end, my Nan died just a few months before my eighteenth birthday, while I was pregnant with my daughter,

Nikitta. I never did find out what she thought she saw that day but, if she really could see my future, maybe it's best she took it to the grave with her.

Because the reality was far worse than anything that carefree, innocent little girl could ever have imagined.

Chapter One

Nikitta

The moment I set eyes on my daughter, I thought she was the most beautiful girl in the world.

When Nikitta was first placed on my chest, I was a little woozy from the pain relief and I struggled to drink in my baby's features: the thin covering of dark hair on her little head; her huge, dark eyes and her wrinkled, newborn skin. But as I rocked her in my arms, holding her tiny pink hands in mine, everything slowly slid into focus and I felt like my heart might burst with pride. She was mine, really mine: my little girl.

To be truthful, I was only a child myself when I went into labour on the evening of 18 December 1991. My Mum, Jane, had been perming my hair when I'd started to feel a little strange, with short, sharp pains shooting down my back. I was only seventeen and, almost a whole week before my due date, I didn't really entertain the idea that I could be going into labour because I didn't really know what to expect.

In fact, Mum figured out what was going on before I did. I guess it's just a mother's instinct, isn't it? She took one look at me and ordered me upstairs, where she ran me a hot bath.

'You're in labour, Marce,' she told me, her tone very matter-of-fact.

I hadn't expected to fall pregnant so quickly when I'd met Paul Brunnock just over a year beforehand. I hadn't paid him much attention when we'd first locked eyes at a party in a house near both of our family homes on the Ringland estate in Newport, South Wales, although I noticed he was handsome, with a cheeky smile and big brown eyes. I could sense the same brown eyes lingering on me long after I'd turned away and, at the end of the night, he asked if he could walk me home. Stubbornly, I refused.

'I think I'll manage on my own,' I replied. 'But thanks.'

'Oh, you're a bit of a mouthy one, aren't you?' he said. His eyebrow was raised and, although he was smiling, my face was deadpan.

It was surprising that we hadn't got to know each other before, really. We'd actually played together as babies when we both lived in a bustling part of town called Baldwin Street, which was filled with shops and rows of terraced houses, but, of course, we were too young to remember anything about that time.

Still, both of our families had lived in Newport for generations. Paul was from a big, close-knit family, the second of five boys. His brother, Michael, was eighteen months older than him and he was followed by Matthew, Andrew and Richard. They left Baldwin Street just before I moved to a part of town called Lliswerry with my Mum, Jane, and my Dad, Terry.

Neither of us came from flush backgrounds and times could often be tough but our parents were real grafters and worked their fingers to the bone to provide for us. My Dad worked at the local Llanwern steelworks and Mum juggled various jobs, catering and cleaning for lots of different companies. Paul's mum was a cleaner too, while his dad was a bit of an odd-job man, going wherever the work was and trying his hand at everything from gardening to decorating over the years.

After our first meeting, Paul asked to walk me home each and every time we met but I always refused. I'd always been feisty and independent and I saw no reason why I couldn't make my own way home, as we lived in opposite directions anyway. By this point, we had a lot of mutual friends so our paths often crossed at parties. Paul was a bit of a loveable rogue and, like most teenage boys, always seemed to be in some sort of scrape. One evening, he flashed me his trademark cheeky smile and I suddenly felt myself softening a little.

'So, Marce,' he said. 'Are you ever going to let me walk you home?'

He must have asked me dozens of times, and dozens of times I'd said no but this time I felt the corners of my mouth twitching and, before I knew it, I'd broken into a little half-smile.

'Just this once, then,' I agreed.

We shared our first kiss that night but it was a while before I properly opened up to Paul. I suppose I was sizing him up; trying to figure him out before I let him in. I've always been slightly cautious around strangers and I didn't want to dive headfirst into anything, young and carefree though we both were.

In time, though, we became a proper couple. We were really young and we rarely had money to go on dates to pubs and the cinema, so we mainly met at friends' houses, or sometimes I'd sneak Paul into Mum and Dad's.

We'd only been together a few months when Paul asked me to marry him. He didn't go down on one knee and there was no way either of us could have afforded a ring but his expression was deadly serious as he turned to me one night when we were walking home from a party.

'How would you feel about getting engaged, Marce?' he said, knotting his fingers through mine.

I don't think he got the reaction he'd been hoping for because I burst out laughing.

'Paul, you have to be joking!' I replied. 'We've only just met!'

'I'm not joking!' he insisted. 'I really mean it.' Soon, though, he was giggling too. Once I'd decided against something, there was rarely any talking me round. I have a real stubborn streak.

I know that some girls might have been swept away by the romance of it all but I've never been one for fairytales and I've always tried to keep my feet on the ground. I suppose by then I was starting to fall in love with Paul but I was realistic.

I'd just turned seventeen and he was barely six months older than me. Anything could happen and it would be silly to stand in front of all of our family and friends, pledging to be together forever, when we still had so much living to do. Plus, I've always hated being the centre of attention. The idea of standing in the middle of a big room in a puffy white dress with everyone's eyes on me filled me with absolute horror. It still does, if I'm honest.

Nonetheless, as streetwise and savvy as I thought I was, I was about to be catapulted spectacularly into adulthood.

Sometime around the spring of 1991 I started to feel a little off-colour. I was being sick a lot and I assumed I just had a bad tummy bug but, when the nausea wouldn't subside, I went to see the doctor.

'Congratulations,' he told me. 'You're three months pregnant.'

I almost collapsed with shock. I was only a child myself and I had no idea how I would cope with being a mum. Paul was much calmer than I was and he even seemed quite excited at the prospect of being a dad – but I was terrified.

The doctors couldn't work out exactly when I'd conceived, so I was given a few different due dates. Eventually, they seemed to agree on 24 December – Christmas Eve. I'd imagined I'd be spending the festive season going to parties and socialising with friends. It was quite something to think I'd be preparing for the birth of my first child.

Paul's parents took the news in their stride but Mum and Dad were a bit more shocked. Neither of us was yet eighteen and we had no grasp on the reality of parenthood.

'What about marriage?' Mum said, echoing the question Paul had asked me just a few months beforehand. 'Does he want to get engaged? Is he serious about you?'

I knew Paul was serious about me – or, if he wasn't, he was good at pretending he was – but I just shrugged and said nothing. Overnight, our carefree walks home across Ringland felt like ancient history.

'You should do things the right way,' Dad agreed. 'Get a house, get married. It will be better for the baby.'

I just sat on the couch, virtually dumbstruck. I couldn't get my head around having a child because I was just a child myself.

The rest of my pregnancy passed in a bit of a blur. It was so surreal, thinking that there was a little boy or girl growing inside of me and, as Nikitta started to move around in my womb, I could barely contemplate the idea of being a mother, of being responsible for another little person.

Mum and Dad tried their best to help prepare me for motherhood. Their initial reservations soon faded to excitement as they contemplated the prospect of having their first grandchild. They even let Paul move in for a while, until we found somewhere more permanent to start family life.

Not that either of us coped well with being under their roof and subject to their rules. As lots of seventeen-year-olds do, we thought we were already fully-grown adults and we hated being under any kind of scrutiny. Halfway through my pregnancy, we decided to move in with some friends who had a flat a few streets away, on the other side of Ringland.

At first, it was great to have a bit of freedom but, even in

6

my youthful naivety, I realised it wasn't going to work out in the long term. Our friends were barely older than us and they wanted to party all the time, which is understandable, really. Of course, at seventeen, I was legally too young to drink but it had never stopped me before. But, pregnant and sober as everyone got drunk around me and my bump grew bigger by the day, the parties weren't so much fun.

I sort of found my way back to Mum and Dad's. Paul stayed over quite a bit but at other times he stopped with various family members. We knew we'd have to find a place of our own when the baby came along but our makeshift arrangements would do until then.

As it happened, 18 December 1991 was Paul's eighteenth birthday and he'd gone out to celebrate in some of the local pubs with our friends. It was in the days before mobile phones, so I couldn't call him to let him know the baby was on its way.

As I soaked in the warm bath Mum had run for me, the pains in my back and stomach slowly became stronger and more regular. I dried myself off and climbed into some fresh clothes. As soon as I got downstairs, Mum started quizzing me on my contractions and how often they were coming. I don't remember being in agony or anything, it was just a bit uncomfortable.

'I think the baby is coming soon,' she said. 'We'll need to get you to hospital. And where the hell is Paul?'

I shrugged. 'He's out. It's his birthday, remember?'

Neither Mum nor Dad had a car, so Mum rang for an ambulance to take me to the Royal Gwent Hospital. It had just drawn up outside the gate when a taxi pulled in behind it and Paul came stumbling out, slightly worse for wear.

'What's going on?' he asked, wide-eyed.

'Hurry up! Marce is in labour,' Mum said. 'We're going to the hospital now.'

Paul did as she said and we all piled into the back of the ambulance. As it happened, one of my friends who had been out with Paul celebrating his birthday had told him off for being out late when I was so close to giving birth. With impeccable timing she'd taken his drink off him and bundled him into a taxi.

We arrived at the hospital just after midnight on 19 December and I was given some gas and air as pain relief. Neither Paul nor I fully grasped the seriousness of what was about to happen. In fact, we were having a bit of a giggle. The gas and air made me hallucinate a bit and I started telling Paul a story about how two little dogs were chasing a chicken round our kitchen! Paul thought it was so funny that he tried some of the gas and air himself, prompting my Mum to slap him round the head for stealing it from me.

I was so out of it that I can barely remember the next few hours but it seemed like no time before Nikitta was in my arms.

'Nikitta,' I said without a moment's hesitation. 'Nikitta Jade.'

Paul didn't argue about my chosen name for a newborn child – we both knew it was a beautiful name. A few years ago I'd decided that, if ever I had a daughter, that's what I'd call her. I'd had a part-time job in a cafe and I'd got chatting to a couple of customers I'd grown to know. The woman had been pregnant and she'd told me that's what she planned to call her baby if it was a girl. I told her there and then that I planned to steal it.

So that's how we found ourselves, little Nikitta Jade and I, on the morning of 19 December 1991. Paul and I spent the next few hours feeding and changing her, taking in every detail of her little face, wondering as all new parents do what kind of girl she would grow into, and dreaming of the songs she'd sing and the games she'd play. Already we were both fiercely protective of her. The idea that she should come to any harm was just unthinkable so, when I laid her on the bed when she was just a few hours old and she began to turn blue around the mouth, both Paul and I were consumed by terror.

Paul ran outside and dragged a nurse to our daughter, practically grabbing her by her blue tabard. The nurse checked Nikitta over and, when she assured us everything was OK, relief coursed through my veins.

'Thank God,' Paul said. I could see the tears glistening in his eyes.

As I held Nikitta to me, taking another glance at her precious, tiny face, my mind had already gone into overdrive. I pictured her toddling around, starting school, making friends and eventually bringing home her first boyfriend. I found it easy to imagine her as a child and even as a teenager. I just knew she'd be gorgeous and I smiled with pride as I thought of her blossoming, turning heads in the street.

But after that, my mind became cloudy. I'm not suggesting I had any kind of premonition about what would happen to her later in life but my imagination just seemed to stall when I tried to picture her as an adult. I couldn't see her on her wedding day, or as a mum herself.

Maybe it was just a coincidence. Or maybe, right from the start, I instinctively knew Nikitta was too beautiful for this world.

Chapter Two
Childhood

*T*here's no denying that the first few years of my life as a new mum weren't the easiest.

We got out of hospital the day after she was born. Six days later she had her first Christmas at Mum and Dad's, though she slept through most of it, tucked away in her little Moses basket. Mum insisted on dipping her dummy in the tiniest bit of gravy so she could say she'd given her granddaughter her first Christmas dinner.

'No!' I squealed. 'You can't do that. She's only supposed to have milk!'

Like most new mums, I was paranoid that anything and everything would harm my baby but, of course, she was fine.

I stayed at Mum and Dad's for a few more weeks but they were both working full-time and it wasn't fair to crowd out their house with a small baby. The council gave me a room in a special hostel for new mums. It was in a street called Clifton Place, near the city centre. I knew we wouldn't be living in the lap of luxury but I consoled myself with the fact that it was a temporary measure until the council found us a proper flat. It was clean, but basic, with bare beige walls and some old-looking furniture. It was OK, I guess. I kept myself to myself and didn't see much of the other mums. I spent most of the day at Mum and Dad's, so I just used it as a place to sleep and, although I'd been told Paul couldn't stay with us at Clifton Place, I used to sneak him in at night and no one really seemed too bothered.

We were only there for a few weeks when I got a call from the council to say a bedsit had become available on Llanthewy Road. I wasn't expecting anything spectacular, but the second I walked through the door I just knew I couldn't live there. It was absolutely filthy and the mouldy walls meant the whole place smelled of damp. There was nothing there but a tatty pair of bunk-beds and pile of dirty socks, abandoned by the previous occupant. Had I been on my own, I might have been able to grin and bear it, but I couldn't stand the thought of Nikitta living in such squalor. I went back to Mum and Dad's for a few days until the council found us somewhere else.

The second bedsit was a slight improvement on the first but it was still pretty grim. It was in the attic of a converted house just across the road from the first bedsit and there were other people living in various parts of the building. I don't think it had ever been decorated. There was a double bed, though, so there was at least room for both Paul and me. My Grancha, Mum's dad, gave us a little cooker so we could make our food in the privacy of our small room. It made things a bit cramped but I was so grateful not to have to navigate the communal kitchen as it was never very clean.

Finally, when Nikitta was seven months old, the council told us they'd found us a little flat. I was so excited at the thought of finally having a home of our own but my joy was tempered with despair when they told me the flat was in Bettws, two bus rides away from Mum and Dad's in Ringland. Anyone who has a baby will understand how much of a challenge navigating public transport with a pram can be.

I'd never really had much reason to go to Bettws before we moved there but it instantly gave me a bad feeling. Back in the early 1990s it had a reputation for being a bit rough. Perhaps it was because I didn't know anyone but it seemed to lack the community spirit of Ringland. Our flat was in a street of drab, forgotten-looking houses and, when I walked across the threshold of our new flat, Nikitta gurgling in my arms, I felt a knot of dread form in the pit of my stomach.

I suppose, looking back, the flat was OK but it was uninspiring. The walls were all painted a dreary magnolia, apart from the kitchen, which was a lurid shade of green. Paul and I barely had a penny to our names, so all of our furniture was second-hand, having been donated by various relatives. Paul's Mum and Dad gave us a huge industrial washing machine and drier, which we were so grateful for. It was so big that it took Paul and one of his mates to carry it in and it made big silver scratch marks on the stairs, although they faded with time.

The days in Bettws were long and lonely. I loved being Nikitta's mum but I soon came to realise how little I knew about life. I'd always loved kids and growing up, I'd done lots of babysitting but being responsible for a little person all on my own was often overwhelming. Very occasionally, if I had a bit of money, I'd take Nikitta into town in her pram and have a look round the shops. I'd all but stopped treating myself though, as I'd much rather have bought a cute little outfit or a toy for Nikitta than anything for myself. Sometimes I could only afford to buy her a small thing from the pound shop but it was better than nothing.

Gradually, Nikitta's black hair lightened and turned a beautiful golden colour. With every day that passed, her chocolate-brown eyes seemed to grow bigger and more alert. My heart swelled with pride when strangers stopped me in the street and remarked on what a gorgeous little girl she was. She was barely a year old, but even then, she stood out.

Perhaps unsurprisingly, Paul and I were fighting a lot. In such a short space of time, we'd gone from being carefree teenagers to fully-fledged adults, responsible for feeding and clothing a child. I suppose it didn't help that we were always skint too.

When Nikitta was around eighteen months old, Paul and I split up. We'd rowed over something so silly I can't even remember what it was now. All I know is that tempers frayed and we decided to go our separate ways. Feeling low following the split, I stayed at Mum and Dad's for a few days with Nikitta, while Paul went off to stay with some friends. All we both needed, in reality, was just a bit of space.

Of course, it wasn't long before Nikitta and I had both run out of clothes, so I had to leave her with Mum and make the trip back to Bettws. It's only about six miles from Mum and Dad's but back then it felt like a million miles away, in more ways than one.

As I pushed open the front door to the flat, my stomach twisted. We had a big wall unit in the living room and the first thing I saw was that the drawers had been pulled out and turned upside down.

It took a few seconds for it to dawn on me that we'd been burgled. At first I thought that Paul had been back to the flat and had simply left it in a bit of a mess. But, as my eyes scanned the room, I slowly realised that everything we owned was gone. The burglars had even taken Nikitta's teddies and the various pictures of family members we'd hung on the walls.

I bit my lip hard and ran into the bedroom to find a similar scene. Panic and bile rose in my throat as I found the wardrobe and all of the drawers bare. Every single outfit I'd scrimped and saved to buy Nikitta had been stolen. I'd also bought her some bedding for when she eventually grew out of her cot: they'd taken the lot. They'd even stolen my underwear. I'd never felt so mortified or violated.

It took me a few seconds to work up the courage to go into the kitchen but, naturally, they'd ransacked that too. They'd even taken the big washing machine and drier.

It was then that the tears sprang to my eyes. It's hard to describe how it feels, losing everything you own. I think it's worse when you didn't have much to start with. A thousand questions were running through my mind but my first thought, as ever, was of Nikitta. How could I ever afford to replace her lost teddies or buy her more pretty clothes? It was just so unfair.

Somehow, I found myself in the middle of the hallway outside the flat and I began to shake as I noticed the freshly made silver scratch marks on the stairs. I hadn't paid any attention to them on the way up but now it was obvious they'd come from our washer and drier because they looked exactly like the marks that had been left when we'd first brought it in.

'Oh, hello,' someone said behind me. The sudden voice startled me and I turned around to see my upstairs neighbour standing beside me. She was a kind, elderly lady, with soft grey hair. 'I thought you'd moved out,' she said. She suddenly paused, no doubt noticing how shaken up I looked. 'Are you OK?' she ventured.

'I haven't moved,' I said hoarsely. 'We've been burgled. They've taken everything. All of my baby's things – everything.'

'Oh, God!' my neighbour said. 'I saw a white van here yesterday. There were a couple of men moving stuff out of the flat. I thought it was a removal van. They even spoke to me. I had no idea. I'm so sorry.'

At first I couldn't believe that the thieves had been so brazen but then I started to piece things together. I've always been a bit of detective and I like to work things out for myself.

One thing I'd quickly learned in Bettws was the names of

people it was best to avoid. There was one man, Tommy, who drove a white van. Always up to no good, he was known for being a bit of a rogue. He lived with a girl around my age and she'd just fallen pregnant. It made perfect sense.

My despair turned to fury as I tore across the estate to the block of flats where Tommy and his girlfriend lived. I only stopped for breath when I was outside their front door. His white van was parked at the side of the road. I peered through the window. On the back seat was one of Nikitta's favourite teddies and leading to the front door of Tommy's flat were the tell-tale scratch marks from my washer and drier.

I just froze for a second, not sure what to do. In the end, I went round to the local police station but the officer on duty wasn't much help.

'I've lost everything!' I said. 'Please – I have proof. Can you speak to them?'

He stifled a sigh. 'I'm sorry, Miss Grender. There isn't enough evidence.'

'But you don't understand!' I went on. 'I have a little girl and they've taken all of her toys and clothes.'

'We'll look into it,' the officer said, though, of course, I knew they probably wouldn't.

It probably wasn't a good idea to confront Tommy and his girlfriend. Everyone knew he was bad news and, had I not been a mum, I might have let it lie but now I was a woman possessed. I couldn't bear the thought of their baby wearing the clothes I'd lovingly bought for Nikitta, or playing with the toys she'd loved so much.

I turned on my heels and ran back to the block of flats where they lived, straight past the white van and the scratch marks on the pavement. As I rattled their front door, I held my breath.

After what seemed like forever, Tommy's girlfriend answered the door. I'm still not sure what her name was. She had a huge baby bump and a sour expression.

'Do you know,' I began, breathless with rage, 'you are washing your clothes in my washing machine?'

'What are you on about?' she said with a sneer.

'Your baby will be playing with my baby's toys and wearing her clothes!' I shrieked. 'You're probably even wearing my bloody underwear! I know what you've done, I'm not stupid!'

Panic flashed across her face for just a second. 'I... I don't know what you mean. I've not got anything of yours.'

'Oh, really?' I said. 'Well, let me come in and take a look. Let's see if *my* washing machine is in *your* kitchen! Go on then, let me in.'

For the next few minutes we screamed at each other. I tried to push past her but she managed to slam the door in my face. Deflated, I went back to the police station but still they told me they couldn't do anything.

After that, I refused to go back to Bettws. Paul stayed at the flat and I went back to Mum and Dad's. It was crowded but it wasn't like I had loads of options. At least they could help me feed and clothe Nikitta. The idea of starting again was soul-destroying especially now I was no longer with Paul.

Gradually, though, Paul and I started to talk again. He doted on Nikitta and he wanted to see her all the time, so we had to be in touch a lot. Even now it brings a lump to my throat picturing them together in the first few years of her life. Nikitta was Paul's pride and joy and, in turn, she absolutely idolised him. Even as a baby, her big brown eyes would light up the second he walked into the room and picked her up for a cuddle.

I suppose Paul and I just kind of fell into the habit of seeing each other again and soon we were back together. I had one condition, though.

'We can't live in the flat,' I said. 'We'll have to find somewhere else. I hate Bettws now, it's just got too many bad memories.'

In truth, I was terrified of scraping together some clothes and furniture only to have Tommy – or someone like him – take them from us again. I spoke to the council and, eventually, a flat became available on Stanford Road, just a few streets away from where Mum and Dad lived.

'I'll take it,' I said without hesitation. I hadn't even seen it but I didn't need to. It would have to do.

'It's a top-floor flat,' the lady at the council told me. 'Not ideal if you have a baby and a pram. I don't want to put you off – I'm just saying.'

But I didn't care. I was just so happy to be back in Ringland, with a proper chance for the three of us to start a life together as a little family.

Of course, the flat was far from a palace. The furniture looked like something from the 1970s and the wallpaper was a horrible combination of purple, brown and gold. There were only two little bedrooms but that was all we needed.

'We'll do it up nicely,' Paul said. 'Bit by bit.'

And we did. We decorated the living room first, papering the walls in a nice light burgundy, with curtains to match. Then we did Nikitta's room up in pink, before moving on to our own bedroom, which we painted a silvery blue. It mightn't have been grand but it was our home and it was perfect.

That said, sometimes I wonder if our flat was haunted because during our time there Nikitta often talked about a woman who came to play with her at night when we'd all gone to bed and there were times when we heard footsteps on the stairs, only to discover no one was there. Nikitta never seemed threatened or scared, though: she took it all in her stride.

As she grew into a toddler, she became more and more beautiful by the day: her brown eyes got bigger and her hair turned golden. Her lips were so full and pink that it looked like they'd been tinted. At first I thought it was just me who was captivated by her, as every mother thinks her children are gorgeous, doesn't she? But I lost count of the number of strangers who stopped in their tracks as we passed them on the street, marvelling at how lovely she was.

'Look at those eyes!' they'd say. 'Isn't she beautiful? And so well behaved.'

'She's like Daisy Cow, with those big brown eyes,' my Grancha used to say, beaming with pride. 'And such a good girl.'

It was true: Nikitta was so respectful and polite around strangers. I think it was because she was so used to being in the company of adults. As Paul and I were so young, few of our friends had children for her to play with and she didn't yet have many cousins. She always said 'please' and 'thank you' and did as she was told, at least when in the company of others. When she was home alone with me, it was a different story.

I suppose, from the start, Nikitta and I were more like sisters than mother and daughter. I was so young that I wasn't sure how to discipline her properly and I probably let her get away with more than I should have. She might have listened to orders from her grandparents and other adults but she often defied me.

I came up with some little songs, which I used to sing to her. Holding her in my arms and humming them in her ear over and over again is one of my most precious memories, painful though it is to recall.

Just before Nikitta started at infants' school, she became obsessed with Mr Blobby. She'd giggle so much when he came on the TV that it made Paul and me laugh too. She insisted we get her Mr Blobby curtains and bedding.

It was around this time that Paul found a job in a windscreen-wiper factory. For the first time since we'd had Nikitta, we had a little bit of money – not much but enough for an occasional toy or a treat. Things were finally looking up.

Nikitta started at Ringland Primary School in the September of 1995 and she took to it like a duck to water. She loved being around other children and she made lots of friends. She was never keen on the academic side of things, though. From as early as five years old, I remember her refusing to do her homework or go through her reading books.

'You're not my teacher, you can't make me,' she'd say with a grin. From an early age, she was more interested in dressing up and stealing my make-up than in sums and spelling tests but I guess that's not unusual for a child of her age.

Not all of her fashion choices were memorable for the right reasons, though. When Nikitta was six, her obsession with Mr Blobby gave way to a fascination with the Spice Girls. She wanted to look exactly like them and begged me to buy her ungainly thick platform shoes and put her hair up in a high ponytail, stuck right in the middle of her head, which I thought looked awful.

'Do I look like Mel C?' she'd ask, hopefully, and I'd just laugh. She was desperate for her hair to grow, so sometimes she'd stick a pair of my black tights on her head and insist I pretend it was her hair. We bought the first Spice Girls album for her on cassette, as was the fashion back then. However, we regretted it almost instantly as she played it over and over and over again. Even now, I could probably recite all of the lyrics to 'Wannabe' off by heart!

It was around this time that I fell pregnant with Luke. I'd been shell-shocked for most of my first pregnancy but this time I was really excited. Paul and I now had a bit of money coming in and a home of our own. We were much better prepared.

I was so happy when Luke was born, as I'd always wanted one girl and one boy. It felt like our family was complete. It was a bit of a shock for Nikitta, though. She'd been used to having me all to herself for six years and at first she viewed her new little brother with suspicion, stealing his dummies and hiding them all over the house.

Luke was around six months old when we were given a three-bedroom council house in Broadmead Park, just a ten-minute walk from Ringland. We were delighted as it meant Nikitta and Luke would have a room each.

From the second we walked through the door, it felt like home. Despite everything that has happened in our lives, even to this day we've refused to leave the house because it holds so many happy memories for us of both of our children.

When Luke went off to nursery, I began volunteering at Ringland Primary School. I'd always loved working with young people and, eventually, I was offered a job there as a teaching assistant. I was over the moon. Now both of my children were that bit older, it was nice to have a job and to make some new friends. Of course, the money came in handy too.

Nikitta quickly made friends in Broadmead Park, as she always did, and she was off out playing with them. With Luke, I'd been more prepared for motherhood and I'd always laid the ground rules, but with Nikitta, it was like that ship had sailed. She was a bit rebellious because she'd been able to get away with more than she should have as a little girl. She never did anything drastic but I saw a lot of myself in her. Stubborn and independent, she liked you to think she didn't need you.

As she grew older, no one could deny how beautiful she was. Even towards the end of primary school, I'd catch the boys in her class staring at her. It made Paul a bit uneasy. I suppose fathers always are when it comes to their little girls.

Nikitta knew she was stunning, though. She couldn't walk past a mirror without looking at herself or fixing her hair. I'd tease her sometimes but I never gave her too much of a hard time. She was bloody gorgeous; she had every right to stare at herself in the mirror!

By the time she started at Hartridge High School, her hair had got a little darker and it was now a deep, mahogany-brown. It just seemed to bring out her big eyes even more. When she started secondary school, she became obsessed with fashion and make-up and she was always experimenting with clothes. Everything looked fantastic on her because she had the perfect size-six figure. Even if she sat on the couch all day and stuffed her face with junk food, she wouldn't gain a pound.

She would sometimes tell me about boys and there was this one lad, Steven, whom she called her boyfriend for a bit. They'd been in junior school together and sometimes they'd leave school at the end of the day holding hands but it was all very innocent. He never came round to the house or anything. Not that Paul or I minded that we never met Steven on home ground. As far as we were concerned, there was plenty of time for Nikitta to find a boyfriend, especially one she was serious enough about to take home to meet the parents.

Sometimes, when I caught her curling her hair or slicking

on mascara instead of doing her homework, I told her she should concentrate on school.

'Stick in and get some qualifications, Keet,' I told her. 'You won't regret it.'

'Whatever, Mum,' she'd say with a sigh.

'I mean it,' I'd say, as sternly as I could.

'How many times do I have to tell you?' she'd reply, sweeping her hair to the side of her head as she peered in the mirror. 'You're my Mum, not my bloody teacher! Anyway, I want to be a hairdresser. You don't need to do maths for that.'

I had to admit, she knew how to make the most of her looks – as if she wasn't beautiful enough already!

She always had lots of friends but her closest mates were Jenna, Shanna, Nicole and Luke, who all lived near us on Broadmead Park. Like any teenager does with their close friends, she spent a lot of time with them, often in town or just hanging out on the estate.

By the time Nikitta was fifteen, she was turning heads as she shimmied round the estate in her little dresses.

'Call that a dress?' Paul would mutter. 'Where's the rest of it?'

Of course, it was only a matter of time until one of the boys whose heads she'd turned caught her attention too. Like any mum, I was apprehensive about who it would be. Teenage boys can be so fickle and I dreaded the day she'd have her heart broken for the first time.

Soon, however, turning a boy's head would spark a chain of events that would change the course of our lives forever.

If only we could turn back the clock.

Chapter Three

Ryan

I suppose Ryan and I didn't get off to the best of starts. Nikitta was fifteen when she met him. I think they were introduced at a party but I can't be sure exactly as, of course, teenagers rarely tell you much about their personal lives. By this point, Paul and I had decided to give Nikitta a little bit of freedom. She was allowed out with her mates but she had a strict 9.30pm curfew on school nights.

By the summer of 2007, with her sixteenth birthday fast approaching, she'd started to push her luck a bit, coming in later than she was supposed to, but I guess all young people try to bend the rules sometimes.

One particular night when Nikitta was tucked up in bed at her normal time, I was just dozing off when somebody threw a rock at one of our windows. I turned over, thinking it must have been an accident, but it was followed by another and another.

'Keeta,' a voice shouted from below. 'Keeta!' The sound of Nikitta's muffled voice travelled through from the other room.

'Sssh!' I heard her say. 'My mum and dad will hear!'

Annoyed, I opened the curtains to see a teenage boy standing on the path below. He had a big quilt wrapped around him and there were two other boys standing behind him. He looked as though he was Nikitta's age, maybe even younger, with mousy-brown hair and angular features. As it was after 10.30pm, my first thought was to wonder why someone so young was roaming the streets so late.

I opened the window and stuck my head out, looking him up and down.

'Excuse me?' I said. I had to raise my voice so he could hear me. 'Who are you?'

'I'm just speaking to Nikitta,' he shouted back. 'I wanted to know if she was coming out, that's all.'

I was gobsmacked. Not only was he unrepentant for throwing stones at our window late at night but he was brazen enough to ask if Nikitta was coming out.

'Of course she's not coming out!' I thundered. 'She's got school in the morning and so do you, I would imagine!'

He shouted something back about not going to school but I'd already slammed the window shut and gone back to bed. The next morning I was on the warpath.

'So, last night, the boy was throwing stones at our window,' I said to Nikitta. 'Who the hell is he?'

'Oh, Ryan?' she replied, casually. 'We've just kind of been seeing each other.'

'You've kind of been seeing each other?' I echoed. 'And how old is this Ryan?'

'He's fourteen,' she said, 'a year younger than me. Why is that important?'

I took a deep breath. I didn't want Nikitta to feel like she couldn't confide in me but something inside me had disliked Ryan from the word go. Perhaps it was just the mother in me, thinking no one would ever be good enough for my little girl.

'OK,' I replied, slowly. 'He's not from round here, is he? I've never seen him before. Where does he live?'

'Oh, his mum's thrown him out,' Nikitta said. 'He's stopping with his auntie.'

I felt my blood pressure rising. Of course, I didn't know if Ryan had actually been thrown out by his mum. It could very well have been teenage bravado but it did nothing to convince me he wasn't a total tearaway.

'Oh, I see,' I said. 'And why has he been thrown out then? There must be a good reason.'

'Oh, I don't know, Mum!' Nikitta snapped. 'Just leave it, right?'

I said no more that day but soon Nikitta was spending more and more time with this Ryan. Although she still saw Jenna, Shanna, Nicole and Luke, they called round less than they used to. Her phone was always glued to her hand and she'd spend entire afternoons moping around, only perking up when Ryan got in touch.

It made me mad and I wouldn't have Ryan in the house. Not only did I think Nikitta was too young to be in such a serious relationship, I felt Ryan was messing her around and that upset me. Nikitta could have had any boy she wanted yet he had the audacity to keep her hanging. It really riled me up. Who did he think he was?

In my more rational moments, I told myself he was a teenage boy and that I was being too harsh. But I couldn't help myself: he just seemed like bad news and I didn't want Nikitta mixed up with him and his silly little friends, as they roamed the streets long after they should have been in bed.

'I don't like him,' I told Paul. 'Do you? There's something about him.'

But Paul was a bit softer than I was and tried to be reasonable.

'Come on, Marce,' he said. 'He's just a young lad. Remember what I was like at that age? He'll grow up.'

'Do you think this is just a phase?' I said. 'She'll grow out of it, surely. She'll soon see she's too good for him.'

Paul just laughed and told me I should give Ryan a bit of a chance. Perhaps he was right but I just couldn't – he really got my back up. Soon, I was thinking of ways to keep Nikitta from seeing him. If she came home a second later than her curfew, I'd ground her, but only because I thought it would force them apart.

It sounds over the top, I know, and it only made Nikitta more determined to defy me. She'd always been like me in that respect – stubborn to the core. At night she'd sneak out to spend time with him and one day, when I'd been sent home from work as I was feeling ill, I caught them snuggled up on the sofa in the living room. I don't think I've ever recovered from an illness so quickly – I chased him out and all the way down the street.

It was around this time that all the teenagers on the estate started logging on to a website called Bebo. It was before everyone had Facebook and Nikitta and her mates loved going on it to share pictures and gossip about what they'd been up to. She was always taking selfies and uploading them.

Soon, though, she'd deleted her page. She said it was causing too many problems, as she claimed one of her friends had tried to chat up Ryan on it. I was a little bit worried as I thought it might mean she would miss out.

'Be careful not to cut off your friends now you have a boyfriend,' I told her but she didn't pay much attention. The girls and Luke – 'Big Luke', as we called him, so as not to confuse him with our Luke – still called round but I could tell they were getting frustrated when I always had to tell them she was with Ryan.

'I'm scared she'll lose her friends,' I confided in Paul. 'They won't hang around forever if she doesn't make the effort.'

'Things will work out, Marce,' he assured me. 'It's her first boyfriend, she's just young. It will be fine.'

But I wasn't so sure. After Nikitta and her friends turned sixteen, most of them left school and got jobs, which meant they had a bit of money to go out to pubs and clubs. At first Nikitta did a few shifts in a hairdresser's but she got bored as she wasn't allowed to do anything but sweep the floor and make tea and coffee. I suggested she go to college and train to be a hairstylist but she'd never liked studying and the thought of three more years of classes put her off. Instead, she enrolled with an agency and soon had a job in a New Look shop, in the retail park just across from our estate. She loved it, especially as it meant she got a discount on all of the clothes.

I had hoped that with a little money of her own she might socialise more but everything still revolved around Ryan. Often, she would mope around the house, staring at her phone, waiting for him to call.

'Why don't you give Jenna a ring, Keet?' I said one day. 'Or Shanna? See if they're going into town?'

She shrugged. 'Maybe.'

'Come on,' I coaxed her. 'Wouldn't it be fun to get dressed up and go out dancing? You could wear one of your new dresses from work.'

'I'm not in the mood,' she said. 'I've made plans with Ryan.'

I inhaled sharply. 'Well, he's not here now, is he? Why don't you have a night with the girls instead, eh? That will be much more fun than just sitting around here.'

'I told you, Mum, I'm not in the mood,' she snapped.

'What time was he meant to be coming round?' I asked.

'Oh, I'm not sure,' she replied. 'He's probably out with his stupid cousin. I can't stand him, he gives me the creeps.'

'His cousin?' I said. 'Who's his cousin?'

'His name is Carl,' she replied. 'He's a bit older. He's horrible, I hate the way he looks at me. And he's always taking Ryan away from me. It's like we're not allowed a minute to ourselves.'

I suppose that was the first time she mentioned Carl Whant, but a few weeks later, I soon forgot about him as she told me she and Ryan had split up. Of course, I did as all mums would and gave her a shoulder to cry on. As much as we fought, she always confided in me when it really mattered and I liked that. Secretly, though, I was quite happy: I really hoped this would mean she'd go out and have fun with her friends and do all of the things teenagers should do. I suppose, in a way, I wanted her to have the youth I never had myself. I wouldn't have changed having her for the world, but our lives had been really hard in the early days, counting every penny just to get by. I wanted Nikitta to wait a while before settling down and to get everything out of her system and maybe get a little bit of money behind her first. Plus, I didn't want her to settle down with Ryan. It might sound bad but I didn't think he had many prospects. He never seemed to go to school, even though he was still only fifteen. I just thought it all seemed like a recipe for disaster.

'I know it might feel horrible now,' I told her. 'But I promise you'll get over this. You'll find someone else, no problem.'

'I don't want to find someone else,' she said, pulling her cardigan around her for comfort.

'Look at you, Keet,' I said. 'You're stunning. Who wouldn't want you?'

It was true. Even as she sat on the couch, with no make-up, a tear-stained face and her hair scraped back, she was beautiful. Sometimes I caught a glimpse of her out of the corner of my eye and marvelled at how I'd managed to produce someone so gorgeous.

'I've got an idea,' I said. 'Why don't you get back on Bebo?'

'What do you mean?' she asked.

'You know – get in touch with all your mates,' I said. 'Arrange a big night out.'

'Nah,' she replied. 'I can't be bothered.'

Eventually, she did stop moping around all of the time, though I could tell she was still pining for Ryan. But, gradually, she began to see more and more of the girls and Luke.

When Nikitta got dressed up, she was even more of a knockout than usual. She had this one little white dress, which really showed off her figure, and I could just imagine how many men must have tried to chat her up when she went out in it.

'Hey, what about that guy from last night then?' Shanna said one night as they were lounging on our couch together.

'Oh, who's this then?' I asked.

'Oh, no one, Mum,' Nikitta said. 'It was nothing.'

'He totally fancied her,' Shanna said, giggling. 'He kept asking for her number!'

'Oh, really?' I said but I could tell Nikitta was getting embarrassed, so I decided to stop quizzing her. I was really glad, though, that she seemed to be having a little bit of fun.

My happiness was short-lived, though, because a few weeks later Ryan was back on the scene. My heart sank as I watched them walking towards the house, hand in hand.

'Have you made up?' I asked Nikitta later on.

'Yes,' she said with a grin. I had to turn around so she wouldn't see the disappointment in my eyes. I don't know what was wrong; I just had this strange sense of foreboding, like nothing good could come of Ryan or the people he hung around with. Maybe I was being judgemental but a mother's instinct is a powerful thing.

The next day, she announced she wanted to move out. I nearly spat out my coffee.

'Move out?' I said. 'And with what money, Keet?'

'Ryan thinks we should get a flat,' she said. 'It's serious this time. We want to spend the rest of our lives together.'

'You're only sixteen!' I protested. 'There's a big world out there. What's the rush?'

'I love Ryan,' she said. 'Why can't you see that?'

Suddenly, an awkward thought entered my mind. No parent likes to think of their teenager having a sexual relationship but it would have been naive of me to believe Ryan and Nikitta weren't sleeping together.

'Keet, are you being – you know – *careful*?' I asked.

'Mum!' she said. 'Stop it.'

Later on, however, we had a proper chat about the subject and we agreed that I'd take her to the doctor so she could have the contraceptive implant fitted. It was supposed to last for three years, so it helped put my mind at rest.

It didn't stop Nikitta from wanting to move in with Ryan, though. One day she disappeared with some bin bags full of clothes and Paul and I realised they'd gone to stay at Ryan's mum's.

I spoke to a few people and I managed to find out where

the house was. It was only then I discovered that Ryan had grown up on the Malpas estate, not far from Bettws. I didn't know what his family would be like, but when I called at the house, his mum was really reasonable. She was called Kerry and she had a few young children, so her house was pretty crowded with an extra person living in it.

'I can't imagine you need another teenager slobbing around,' I said. 'Probably best if she comes home.'

'You're right,' Kerry said. 'It's probably best if they're both at home.'

Nikitta huffed a little for a few days but she seemed to get over it when I relented and told her she could have Ryan round to the house. Little did I know that she was already plotting her next escape. A few weeks later I came home from work to find the house empty. It wasn't unusual, as Nikitta spent nearly every waking hour with Ryan, but when I went to change the bin liner, I found that all of my black bin bags had disappeared from the cupboard. I had a funny feeling I already knew where they'd gone.

I tore up to Nikitta's room, taking the stairs two at a time, and threw open her bedroom door. Her quilt was gone from her bed and none of her clothes were in the wardrobe. Seething, I ran back down to the living room, where she'd quickly scribbled a note and left it on the table.

'I've gone, it's better this way,' she'd written. 'See you whenever, love you loads.'

I grabbed my mobile and dialled Paul's number. By now, he'd got a new job driving a van and he always got in later than me but he was obviously on the road because it rang out. He got home around an hour later to find me pacing the floor. I'd already phoned Nikitta several times but, of course, she'd ignored me.

'She's bloody left home again,' I said the second Paul walked through the door, before he'd even had a chance to say hello. 'It's him. I could have both of them.'

'Just keep calm, Marce,' Paul said. 'She'll come back.'

'No, she won't!' I insisted. 'You must know how bloody stubborn she is.'

The corners of Paul's mouth twitched. 'I wonder where she gets that from, eh?' he said. 'Look, don't worry. Give her a couple of days. Wait until she's run out of food and clean towels and she'll soon come running back.'

I wasn't holding out much hope. Like I said before, I've always been a bit of a detective and I made some inquiries. I heard on the grapevine that she and Ryan were staying in a flat on a street called Corporation Road. It wasn't far from us, so my friend took me along there in her car.

Like a woman possessed I rattled on the door until a dishevelled-looking bloke answered. I could hear music pounding on the sound system inside and the putrid smell of damp wafted out.

'Where's Nikitta?' I asked.

'Eh, Nikitta?' he answered. 'She's not here.'

'I'm not stupid,' I said. 'If you don't bring her out, I'll come in there and get her myself.'

'She's not here,' he repeated. 'Honestly, she's not.'

I barged past him and through the living room just in time to see Nikitta running out of the back door and down an alleyway. The flat was in a terrible state, with wallpaper peeling from the walls and huge patches of mould everywhere, but I didn't have much time to take in my surroundings. I sprinted through the living room, where about half a dozen of Ryan's friends were gathered, and ran after Nikitta. I was on a mission, so it didn't take me long to catch up with her.

'Get home!' I said. 'Now!'

'Why have you got to ruin everything?' she snapped back. 'I'm sixteen, I'm happy here. Why is that so hard to deal with?'

'How can you be happy here, Keet?' I said. 'You have a lovely home and you want to live in this minging flat? I just don't get it.'

I got her home that time, but after that, I knew I was fighting a losing battle. Nikitta was so headstrong that I knew I'd never be able to keep her at home forever. For the next year or so she flitted between home and staying with Ryan at some flat he'd managed to find.

She still liked her home comforts though and no matter where she was staying, she'd always turn up on a Saturday morning for a fry-up, or on a Sunday for a roast dinner.

I suppose it was around then that I softened towards Ryan a bit. I let Nikitta bring him to family parties and I included him in our little weekend rituals. He still spent loads of time with his mates – especially his cousin, Carl – and Nikitta was often home alone. This would have annoyed me if it wasn't for the fact she'd usually come home, wanting to spend time with me so she had some company.

One night we were watching *EastEnders* when I instinctively took her hand in mine.

'Mum, what are you doing?' she said and laughed. 'Stop being a twat!'

But she was smiling and I was smiling, too. 'No matter how old you get, you'll always be my baby,' I said.

'You know those songs you used to sing to me when I was little?' she said. 'Can you sing them now?'

My eyes lit up. 'You really want me to sing to you?'

'Yes,' she said. 'Just sing to me. It's funny.'

I did as she said. When I finished, we both started laughing.

But, while we laughed, I felt a bit wistful. Part of me wished Nikitta was still the little golden-haired girl who wore tights on her head and giggled at Mr Blobby. Now she was almost an adult herself but it was like she was slipping through my fingers.

That night, as I lay in bed, I thought about how I'd dreamed of Nikitta's future when she was a little girl. Now she was the beautiful young woman I'd always imagined she'd be. I still couldn't see her on her wedding day or with children of her own and I certainly couldn't picture her in her thirties or forties. It was impossible to imagine her ageing or looking any different to how she did now.

I told myself I was just being silly, especially as Nikitta seemed to have the rest of her life mapped out.

'I want to get married but I want a baby first,' she said. 'I've thought about my wedding day. I'd want my first child to walk down the aisle with me. That would be nice, wouldn't it?'

'There's plenty of time for that, Keet,' I replied. 'You don't need to be in any rush.'

But, of course, there was no telling her. A few weeks later she came round to the house and she was wearing a ring on her middle finger. My eyes fixed on it as soon as she walked through the back door. It was nothing special – I knew Ryan couldn't afford a real diamond or anything – but my insides somersaulted all the same.

'Keet,' I began, 'is that an engagement ring?'

'Oh, yeah,' she replied, breezily. 'I was going to tell you. Ryan bought me it.'

I shot Paul a look but he changed the subject. Later, when Nikitta had gone, he tried to reassure me about the situation.

'Marce, they're young,' he said. 'Think what we were like. I asked you to marry me when we were that age, didn't I?' With a chuckle, he added, 'And we're still not married.'

'I just assumed it would fizzle out,' I said with a sigh. 'I just don't trust him, Paul. I can't help it. I know he's young but I just think he's holding her back. She should be out experiencing things but she's always hanging around, waiting for him to call her.'

The only thing I could say in Ryan's defence was that he spoiled Nikitta whenever he could. Naturally, he rarely had any money, but if he did have a little bit of cash, he'd spend it on a present for her.

It was a glorious summer evening when we were first introduced to Missy. Paul and I were sitting out in the garden when Nikitta appeared, clutching a tiny pug dog. The puppy was absolutely tiny – barely the size of her hand – and my heart melted the moment I laid eyes on her.

'Look, Mum!' she said. 'Isn't she gorgeous?'

'She's beautiful,' I cooed. 'Whose is she?'

Nikitta grinned. 'Mine,' she said. 'Ryan got her for me. I'm going to call her Missy.'

Suddenly, I hardened. Nikitta was living at home but she had no idea how much hard work was involved in caring for a pet, not to mention how messy they were.

'No, Nikitta,' I said. 'Not in the house, I'm sorry. I don't want any animals.'

Nikitta looked crestfallen. 'Oh, but look at how cute she is!' she said, stroking Missy's tiny head. 'Her mum died and she was the last pup left in the litter. I don't think anyone wanted her because she was so tiny. How sad is that?'

Of course, that absolutely broke my heart but I had to stand firm.

'No, Nikitta,' I repeated. 'We don't have anything for a pup in here. We've got no bedding. You can't bring her in here. I'm sorry, love.'

Just then Nikitta's phone buzzed with a text from Jenna.

'Mum, Jenna's just asked me to pop over,' she said. 'Can I leave Missy here, just for five minutes?'

'Oh, OK then,' I agreed. 'But don't be long.'

I might have known what Nikitta was up to – she was clever like that. She knew that, by the time she'd come back from Jenna's, I'd have totally fallen in love with Missy.

As it was such a hot day, I had taken a glass of water outside with me. Nikitta was barely out of sight when Missy climbed up to try and drink from it. But she was so small, she fell right in!

'Oh, look, Paul!' I said, picking her up and holding her wet fur to my face. 'She's so small!'

Paul rolled his eyes.

'That means she's staying then?' he said with a small smile.

'Oh, how could we get rid of her?' I said, sighing. 'She's so tiny.'

Two hours later Nikitta came bounding back into the kitchen. I had Missy in my arms and, as soon as Nikitta saw my face, she broke into a huge smile.

'I knew you'd love her!' she cried.

'OK,' I said. 'She can stay. But she's your responsibility, Nikitta. And you can't just take her wherever you like. She'll need to have her jabs before she goes anywhere.'

Nikitta was over the moon. If I thought Missy was a bit of a novelty for her, I needn't have worried. From that moment on, they were inseparable. Nikitta treated Missy like a child, buying her little outfits and carrying her around in her handbag.

'Look, it's Paris Hilton!' someone said one afternoon as they walked around Broadmead Park together.

From that moment on, Nikitta was known as 'Paris' to all of our neighbours. She was like a local celebrity, always so glamorous, with her tiny handbag dog. Everyone round our way knew their faces and stopped to say hello. Paul and I thought it was really funny because we knew how much Nikitta loved the attention.

We could never have predicted that one day Nikitta and Missy would be known far beyond Broadmead Park and even Newport.

Chapter Four

Pregnancy

I'll never forget the day I found out Nikitta was expecting Kelsey-May. We'd had another fight, so we hadn't spoken for a few days. She'd left home again and gone to live with Ryan in a horrible flat on Corporation Road, one of the main streets running through Newport. One of his relatives had been renting it but he'd signed the tenancy over to Ryan. I just couldn't understand why she'd want to leave our lovely family home to live somewhere so vile, no matter how much freedom she had. The walls were black with mould and it was on a really rough part of the street. People were always fighting outside and one of the windows had been smashed by a local drunk in a fit of rage.

So when my phone buzzed and I saw I had a message from Nikitta, I expected it would be some sort of half-hearted, teenage apology. I hoped she'd come to her senses, realising that clean towels and hearty dinners don't appear by magic. Either that or she'd be asking for money for a McDonald's. As much as we rowed, however, she never expected much. A couple of quid for a burger and some chips was usually enough to keep her happy.

But when I opened the text, I felt my insides flip.

'Can I come over tonight?' she'd written. 'I need to talk to you.'

Sometimes, when you're a mum, you just know things instinctively, don't you? It's like a sixth sense. She'd already moved out, so she didn't want to speak to me about leaving home – not that she'd seek my approval anyway.

I could tell straight away that she was pregnant. The rest of my classes passed in a blur that afternoon, as I tried to persuade myself I was wrong.

It was another beautiful day, just like when Nikitta had first brought Missy round a few weeks earlier, and Paul and I were out in the back garden. I didn't dare tell him that I thought she was pregnant, as saying it out loud would make it seem far too real. I simply sat on my deckchair, silently seething, staring into the vast expanse of woodland behind our house.

After what seemed like hours, Nikitta appeared around the corner. She showed no signs of a baby bump, her size-six figure perfectly intact in her little shorts and vest top. Missy was on a lead and she was flanked by Ryan and one of his good-for-nothing mates.

Instinctively, I folded my arms as she threw open the gate and I could feel my expression sour.

'So what is it then?' I demanded.

She paused for only a fraction of a second. 'Mum, Dad,' she said. 'I'm pregnant.'

She said it so casually that it was like she'd announced she was popping to the shops for a pint of milk.

Paul's face fell in shock but I didn't move from my deckchair. I could feel the blood rushing to my head. Although I'd guessed her news, it didn't make it any easier to hear it out loud. Sure, I'd been young and foolish when I'd had Nikitta but we'd made a good go of it. We both had jobs and we could provide for our kids. I couldn't help but look at Ryan and wonder what kind of life my precious daughter would be sentenced to now she was permanently tied to him; bound to him by another human being.

'No need to tell me,' I snapped back. 'I already know.'

'How do you—?' Nikitta began.

'Because I'm not stupid,' I interrupted. 'Do you know how difficult it is bringing up a child? Do either of you have any idea?'

Ryan looked sheepishly at the ground but Nikitta met my eye.

'We're happy,' she said defiantly. 'We've thought this through. This is what we want – to be a family.'

'To be a family?' I spluttered. 'You're only children yourselves! He's even younger than you! And you've got no money.'

'This is what we want,' Nikitta said again. She'd gritted her teeth and folded her arms, mirroring my stance.

But I couldn't listen to her any more. Beyond tears, I jumped to my feet and ran back into the house, slamming the door behind me. Perhaps, if Ryan had had some prospects, I'd have been more understanding but the thought of Nikitta and her unborn baby huddled in a damp and rotting flat while he gallivanted with his mates was too much for me to bear. I could just sense she'd be left holding the baby and that was no life for a teenager. At least Paul had mucked in when we'd been in the same position. I was far from confident that Ryan would do the same.

Moments later, Paul came back into the house. Nikitta and Ryan had gone.

'I can't even look at her,' I said. 'I'm so angry. How far along is she?'

'Come on, Marce,' Paul replied, placing his hand on my shoulder. 'We managed. She's only three or four weeks gone.'

'Oh, but look at him, Paul!' I cried. 'She's got no chance. He's got no job, nothing.'

'Oh, Marce,' Paul said. 'Give the lad a break. He's just young. I see a lot of myself in him. Remember what I was like at that age?'

My mind flashed back to Paul and I giggling in the delivery suite as we waited for Nikitta to arrive, him tipsy and stealing my gas and air. Neither of us had any idea of the enormity of what about to happen but we'd coped. You just do when there is no other option. But I couldn't have smiled, even if I had wanted to. I'd wished for better for Nikitta.

'I thought she'd tell me,' I said. I realised now that the tears had sprung to my eyes. 'I'm gutted, Paul. She's always told me everything. I thought she'd tell me if she was going to start trying.'

Paul wrapped me in a hug. 'Of course she's not going to tell you. You'd have tried to stop her! And you know how stubborn she is.'

'But we do share a lot,' I said, sniffing. 'And I thought she'd feel like she could tell me this.'

Suddenly, I remembered the frank conversation we'd had before I'd taken her to have her implant fitted. I'd taken the afternoon off work especially. I'd felt so reassured, knowing she was protected. Now, I felt like a fool.

'She must have had her implant removed,' I said. 'She'll have properly planned this. She thinks she's an adult. Little does she know.'

It pains me to say it now but for weeks I could barely look at her. I didn't want to go round to her flat, as it I didn't want to see the squalor she was living in – it would have broken my heart. Nikitta, being as stubborn as I am, stayed away from home as much as she could too. We barely spoke for some time.

I didn't even think about the fact that I was set to become a grandmother. To be honest, I think I was still in denial. My grandchild wasn't real to me yet. I was still so mad that Nikitta had gone behind my back and got her implant removed after I'd tried to be so supportive.

A few weeks later I finally came to my senses. Paul had been round to visit Nikitta at the flat and she really wasn't very well.

'She's being sick a lot, Marce,' he told me. 'I don't think she's having a very good pregnancy.'

Suddenly, I was filled with remorse. My daughter needed me and here I was holding a grudge against her for getting pregnant.

'Take me round now,' I insisted.

When I knocked on the door of the flat, I had a horrible feeling in the pit of my stomach. It looked even worse than I remembered. The window still hadn't been repaired and, as soon as Nikitta opened the door, the smell of damp almost knocked me out.

My daughter was almost unrecognisable. Gone was the glamorous girl, with her fashionable clothes and make-up. Her skin was blotchy and looked almost grey. Her hair, normally styled to perfection, was scraped into a tight ponytail at the top of her head. Although she was nearly three months pregnant, she was as skinny as a rake. Instinctively, I put my arms around her.

'I feel so rough, Mum,' she said. 'I've had the most awful morning sickness. Well, I don't know why they call it morning sickness when it's all day long.'

'It's OK,' I replied. 'I'm here, now.'

'I've got a really bad cough too,' she admitted. 'I don't know why I'm so run down. I didn't think being pregnant would be this bad.'

It was no wonder she was so ill. I walked through to the living room with her and the walls were even blacker than I had remembered.

'Keet, no wonder you're coughing,' I said. 'Look how mouldy this place is!'

I ran upstairs to take a look in her bedroom. It was

worse. Mould was streaked everywhere, even eating into the mattress on the bed. The bathroom was tiny and I knew Nikitta would never be able to get in and out of the shower when her bump got bigger. I almost gagged as I realised filthy water was leaking from the toilet. The floor was sopping wet.

Nikitta was stood behind me, so she couldn't see the dismay on my face.

I turned to her and said, 'You can't live like this, Keet.'

She folded her arms defensively. 'It's not as bad as it seems. We're fine.'

'You're not, love,' I said, 'you're coughing and spluttering everywhere because of the damp. You have to keep your strength for the baby.'

I asked her for the landlady's number, which she passed over reluctantly. I called the number and tried to tell the landlady about the broken window but she shut me down, claiming Nikitta and Ryan would have to pay for it themselves if they wanted it fixed. She wasn't interested in hearing about the damp either. I was on the phone to her for ages, arguing the toss with her. Eventually, I hung up and dialled the council number, where I asked for the environmental-health department. They came out to do some checks and the level of damp was off the scale.

I wanted nothing more than to wrap Nikitta up and take her home to our nice warm house and look after her but I'd come to realise it wasn't an option. She'd only find a way to leave again. Now that she was pregnant she had even more reason to claim she ought to be allowed to live with Ryan.

Plus, she was fast approaching her nineteenth birthday. I couldn't tell her what to do.

With a heavy heart, I helped them contact the housing department at the council. Because Nikitta was pregnant, they found a flat for them almost straight away. I was reassured a little when I realised it was in Broadmead Park. It needed a bit of doing up but it was a hundred times better than the place they'd been living in.

'I can't wait to decorate the nursery,' Nikitta said with a beaming smile when she stepped across the threshold for the first time.

I think that was the moment when I finally realised how much I longed to be a grandmother. Suddenly I was overwhelmed by the enormity of it all. I couldn't wait to start buying little outfits, to babysit at the weekend and to have someone say the word 'Nanna' to me.

'Do you think it's a boy or a girl?' I asked Nikitta.

'Girl,' she answered immediately. 'But I can't wait to find out for sure.'

Nikitta loved her newfound independence and our relationship was all the better for it. Now I wasn't trying to drag her home, she actually came back of her own accord. Every night, I'd come home from work to hear Missy scratching on the front door as they stood outside waiting for me, Nikitta's neat bump slowly but surely getting bigger.

I was glad she was so close at hand and so was Paul. He helped Nikitta and Ryan with odd jobs around the house. He attempted to show Ryan how to lay some laminate flooring but Ryan's effort was a bit of a disaster and they had to do it all again. But they managed to have a laugh about it. I think they even bonded a little.

I tried my very best to accept Ryan too, knowing he'd soon be tied to our family for good. I invited him for Sunday dinners and for fry-ups on a Saturday, but when Nikitta visited during the week, she was almost always alone, as Ryan and his cousin Carl were inseparable, cruising the streets in Carl's car.

I can't deny it was nice to have some girly time, even if all we did was sit on the couch and watch *EastEnders*, but it did make me worry about how reliable Ryan would be as a dad. It didn't bode well that he spent more time with this cousin than he did with his pregnant girlfriend.

Even after her twelve-week scan Nikitta was still suffering from sickness but I tried my best to keep her strength up with a healthy meal every time she could stomach one. I also sent her home with bags of fruit and vegetables and big bottles of water. Soon I'd started buying Missy a tray of chicken every night as a treat, so she didn't feel too left out. She was so cute that I couldn't help it, even if her hair got everywhere and ruined my lovely clean house!

Then the twenty-week scan came around and we got the news we'd all been waiting for – it was a girl. I'm sure I'd have loved a grandson just as much but I couldn't wait to start buying little pink outfits and things for the nursery.

Decorating the nursery became a bit of a mission for Nikitta and me. I did most of the painting because I didn't like the idea of Nikitta climbing ladders now that she was over halfway through her pregnancy. Everything was pink, of course, and I bought little ballerinas and hearts to stick on the walls. Nikitta loved 'Me to You' bears, so we picked out some bedding from the range and it looked perfect in the baby's little cot.

'Have you thought about names yet?' I asked one night, as we sat at home in front of the telly.

'Yeah, but nothing feels right,' she replied. 'I feel like I'll know the name when I hear it, but I'm just not sure yet what it is.'

I gave her a couple of suggestions but none seemed quite right. Then I had a flash of inspiration. A few years previously, there had been a girl in my class called Kelsey-May. She was beautiful and so sweet and polite. I'd fallen in love with her and when I heard the name, it always made me smile.

'What about Kelsey-May?' I said. 'I like that. It's nice, eh?'

Nikitta's face lit up.

'Oh my God!' she squealed. 'I *love* it! Mum, that's it!'

Every spare penny I had went on the baby. I couldn't go to the supermarket for my weekly shop without picking up a gorgeous little dress or a cute babygro. I also brought practical things, like baby wipes and big bags of nappies. I had never had the money to go all out when Nikitta was small so I wanted to make up for it by really spoiling Kelsey-May.

'She has enough clothes to do her until she's about three!' Nikitta said with a laugh, as I brought home my latest purchase one November evening. It was a beautiful white-and-pink silk party dress, which looked like it had been made for a little flower girl. We had a family wedding planned for the following summer and as soon as I'd seen the dress, I knew it was what I wanted Kelsey-May to wear. Although it looked more suited to a flower girl than a normal guest, I hoped she'd look so beautiful that no one would mind. If Kelsey-May turned out to be anything like her mum, she'd have everyone captivated.

'Don't you think it's gorgeous?' I said when I showed her the dress.

'Oh, yeah,' Nikitta replied. 'I won't let her out in anything that isn't!' She held up another little pink dress I'd picked up in Asda for when Kelsey-May was around six months old. 'I can't wait to see her in this one either! It's lush.'

'I know,' I said with a smile. 'Won't be long.'

'It feels like ages!' Nikitta groaned. 'I just wish she was here. I've still got months to wait.'

She was right. Our granddaughter was due on 21 February 2011, but on those long, autumn nights, it seemed like a lifetime away.

Sometimes, when I lay in bed at night, I tried to picture Kelsey-May. Already she seemed so real to us, especially now we had named her. Would she have Nikitta's big brown eyes, or her beautiful pink lips? I wondered if her hair would be golden like Nikitta's had been when she was a little girl. But, as hard as I tried, I couldn't conjure up an image in my head.

Instead, I thought about the weekends we'd spend together. I remembered being a new mum myself and how grateful I'd been for a break when Nikitta trotted off to either set of grandparents on a Friday night. I was so anxious about Nikitta missing out on the things all young people do, like nights out in the pub and dancing until the early hours with her friends.

'I'll have Kelsey-May on the weekends,' I told Paul. 'Nikitta will want a bit of a break.'

'Every weekend!' Paul said. 'We're mugs, we are.' But he was smiling. He couldn't wait to be a grancha.

Throughout her pregnancy, I encouraged Nikitta to keep in touch with all of her mates. A few of them had started to pass their driving tests, so they'd pick her up in their cars and they'd pop across to the retail park for a McDonald's. Then they'd drive around, listening to music on the radio. They'd never go far – maybe just across to Cwmbran, the next town along from Newport. It was all quite innocent really. As much as I loved having Nikitta round, I knew how important it was for her to have company her own age.

Most nights, though, she'd call round to our place, only leaving when it was time to go to bed. As is often the way with kids when they fly the nest, I saw her far more than I had when she'd lived at home.

'Thank God you're in,' she said one Friday evening as I opened the door and Missy shot through the living room, leaving muddy paw prints everywhere.

'What's wrong, love?' I asked.

'Oh, *he's* there,' she said and sighed. 'Carl. Or "Whanty", as they call him. He's so weird.'

'Can't you tell him to go home?' I asked. 'Tell him you and Ryan would like some time to yourselves?'

'I try,' she said. 'But he doesn't listen. He just won't take the hint. Then he tells Ryan he wants to go out for a drive and they're gone for bloody hours.' She flopped down on the sofa, stroking her bump.

I arched an eyebrow. 'That's not on,' I said.

'I know,' Nikitta went on. 'And, you know, the way he looks at me just makes me feel weird. He's just odd.'

'You know, this will all need to stop when the baby comes along. Ryan can't be out all night, every night, when you have Kelscy-May to look after. It's not fair if he leaves it all to you,' I replied.

Nikitta sighed. 'You'd think, wouldn't you? But Carl has a missus and a couple of kids and he leaves them in the house often enough.' She perked up. 'Ryan won't be like that, though. He's promised me.'

I picked up Missy and sat her on my lap.

'I hope not.'

'He won't be,' she insisted. 'I know he won't.'

A few days later, I met the infamous Carl for myself. He came to the door while I was doing some housework. I was a bit bemused when I opened it, as I'd never seen him before in my life.

'Hello?' I said.

But he just stood there in silence, looking a bit pained. He had a gormless, round face, which was showing the beginnings of a beard.

'Can I help?' I asked, sharply, as he'd still said nothing after a few moments.

'A-are Ryan and N-Nikitta there?' he said eventually. He spoke slowly and carefully, stumbling over a couple of words. Realising he had a speech impediment, I softened a little. I didn't have a clue who he was but I felt a bit sorry for him.

'No, they're not,' I said. 'What's your name? I'll tell them you were looking for them.'

'Carl,' he said again slowly. I could feel my face change as it dawned on me who he was. My sympathy quickly evaporated.

'Oh, well, they won't be back any time soon,' I said. 'Maybe best you ring them tomorrow.' Then I shut the door behind me without another word.

I only met him one more time, during the pregnancy. Paul had invited Ryan round the house to watch a Manchester United v Chelsea game on TV. He was much better at reaching out to Ryan than I was. Although I now included him in family parties and Sunday dinners, Paul made a real effort to get to know him.

'He makes Nikitta happy, Marce,' he told me. 'Let's give the lad a chance and try to get to know him a bit better. He's only a kid.'

But wherever Ryan went, Carl Whant went too. Before I knew it, he was sitting on my couch in the middle of my living room. Nikitta had gone out with one of her friends, thankfully. I can't imagine she'd have been too pleased to find that Ryan's cousin was now hanging around at our place too.

I wasn't happy. I didn't find him threatening. He just struck me as creepy and maybe a little possessive of Ryan. It didn't help that I knew Nikitta didn't like him. But I had no doubt that he fancied her. It might sound biased but it was common knowledge that few men on our estate would knock her back.

While the three of them watched the match, Paul and Ryan growing more animated as the clock ticked past, I sat in the corner of the room, eyes behind my Kindle. I wasn't reading, though – I was watching Carl. He hadn't said a word since he'd come in, or reacted to anything that had happened during the game. Of course, his silence could be put down to his speech impediment but there was nothing to explain his lack of emotion. There wasn't a flicker of it for the whole ninety minutes of the game. It was like his eyes were fixed on a blank screen as he nursed the same can of lager Paul had handed him when he'd first sat down.

Instead, he kept running upstairs to go to the loo. In the space of a few hours he'd gone about ten, maybe twelve times, despite the fact he hadn't finished his first drink.

I didn't know then about his drug habit, of course, but it didn't take a rocket scientist to figure out what was going on. After each of his toilet trips, I went upstairs myself, scouring the bathroom for any traces of cocaine – and checking each of the bedrooms to make sure nothing had gone missing. It sounds awful but I just didn't trust him. Perhaps I had a preconceived idea of what he'd be like because I knew how much Nikitta disliked him but I've always felt like I'm a good judge of character and he really got my back up.

Thinking of the scene now, I always want to vomit: Paul and Ryan, laughing and drinking beer, and him in the background, dead behind the eyes.

As much as he gave me the creeps, I didn't really appreciate how controlling Carl Whant was, especially when it came to Ryan. Ryan didn't have a phone and so, when he went out in the car with Carl for hours on end, Nikitta had no option but to call his cousin if she wanted to know where he was. Whant would often fob her off with excuses, or sometimes just hang up on her.

His hold on Ryan tightened even more when they started working together selling double glazing. It was a double-edged sword. Of course, Nikitta was happy at the prospect of some money coming in, especially as Kelsey-May's arrival was edging ever closer, but she hated the thought of Ryan spending all day with Whant.

One night, just before Kelsey-May was due to arrive, Ryan lost his house keys when he was out with his cousin. The car had got a flat tyre and he'd placed them on the pavement as they changed the wheel. When he went to pick them back up, they were gone.

It remains a mystery where they got to but Ryan was adamant no one could have picked them up in the short time they were changing the tyre. Naturally, I've always wondered if Whant silently pocketed them, grinning his manic, uncouth grin, figuring out when he could put them to good use.

The keys never turned up and Nikitta wasn't best pleased. One night, when Ryan was out with Whant yet again, she turned up at our door. I was a bit bemused to open the door to see her clutching not only Missy's lead but a little baby boy.

'Who's the kid?' I asked.

'Oh, it's his kid,' she replied, taking a seat on the couch. I didn't have to ask who *he* was. 'He brought the baby round with him tonight. Then he took Ryan out again.'

'And left you with his kid?' I said.

'No, I offered,' she said as she bounced the baby on her knee. I had to admit he was really cute but I found myself pitying the poor child, knowing what a waste of space his dad was. 'I knew they wouldn't go far if I had the baby. His missus will be wondering where they've got to if they don't come back soon.'

'What's his missus got to say about this?' I asked. 'She can't be happy, him taking the baby out while he and Ryan go to God knows where. How old is he, six, seven months?'

'About seven months, I think,' said Nikitta. 'His missus doesn't say much. I think she's pretty quiet. She came round to the flat once but she didn't really join in the conversation. She lets him do what he wants, I think. There'll be none of that with Ryan when Kelsey-May is here.'

A few hours passed. I had some housework to get on with, so I watched from afar as Nikitta cooed over the little boy, stroking his hair and tickling him. The delicious sound of baby's laughter filled the house and I could feel myself breaking into a smile as I washed down my kitchen worktops. In just four short weeks Kelsey-May would be here. It wouldn't be long until her laughter filled the house too.

Now I can't even remember what the poor little thing's name was – and even if I could, it probably wouldn't be fair to tell the world. He'll have grown into a boy now. If my maths is right, he'll be at school. He will be just like any of the other innocent little faces I see every day. Newport is a small place and I guess it won't take long for his classmates to figure out his dad is Carl Whant. There's a good chance he'll be mercilessly bullied for something that was never any of his doing. How can any child come to terms with that? How could any parent put them through it?

But I try not to dwell on it when I think of that day. Instead, I think of Nikitta, sitting on the couch, cuddling this little mite, her eyes full of wonder. Her bump was massive now and she looked fit to burst, though she hadn't put on weight anywhere else. Yet she looked so comfortable holding this baby to her, bouncing him gently on her lap as he stared at her adoringly.

I'd had my reservations about her pregnancy; of course I had. I still had nights where I lay awake, worrying about how she'd cope and planning all of the things I could do to help. Raising a child is no walk in the park, after all. Yet, as I saw her sitting on the couch that day, I had to stifle a lump in my throat: she was a natural. I felt silly for doubting myself. She might have been young and naive but she longed for a child and she had so much love to give – we all did.

Her beautiful brown eyes sparkled as she looked up and caught my stare.

'He's gorgeous, isn't he?' she said. 'He needs changing. I thought about bringing some of Kelsey-May's nappies down but they'll be too small. I'd better ring and check where they are.'

Nikitta was so excited about Kelsey-May's arrival that she'd even bought nappies – and lots of them. She handed the baby to me and I nursed him while she was on the phone in the kitchen.

'They're on their way back,' she said as she came back into the living room. Instinctively, she took the baby from me. 'This will be Kelsey-May soon. Can you believe she'll be here in just a few weeks? Though she won't be getting packed off to just anyone when she has a dirty nappy!'

'But you'll be happy to pack her off to me, won't you?' I said jokingly.

She flashed me a cheeky grin. 'You knows you loves me,' she said.

I couldn't help but smile when she said that. She'd started saying it to Paul years ago, when she was just a little kid and she wanted something – usually money for a Happy Meal at McDonald's. Now she said it to us every time she wanted something.

A few minutes later, I heard some brakes screeching to a halt outside the front door. I was glad when Nikitta took the baby out to Whant in the car, rather than inviting him in. He'd never done me any harm but I didn't want him in my house; he set me on edge.

'Daddy's back, Kelsey-May,' she said as the two of them walked back into the house. She was stroking her bump. 'Not long now until we get to meet you.'

Turning to me, she said, 'I just can't wait to be a mummy.'

Chapter Five

The Fire

Saturday, 5 February 2011 dawned a grey and misty day. As I dozed next to Paul I had no idea my world was set to shatter into a thousand tiny pieces. Nothing could have foretold the horrors that were about to unfold. In fact, as Nikitta was just two weeks away from her due date, we were all full of excitement as Kelsey-May's arrival edged closer and my granddaughter's birth dominated my thoughts as I drifted in and out of cosy, peaceful sleep.

As always, Nikitta had been in touch with me throughout the day on the Friday. I had been on my lunch break at work when I'd noticed a text message from her, asking if she could borrow five pounds to go for a McDonald's with her friend Jenna. Instinctively, I'd dialled her number.

'Are you sure you should be going out, Keet?' I said as she answered. 'I'm not sure I like the idea of you going anywhere too far when you're so close to giving birth.'

McDonald's was only a five-minute walk from the estate but Jenna and Nikitta decided to drive there.

'I'll be fine, Mum,' she replied. 'It's my last night of freedom, remember? I'll have plenty of time to stay in when Kelsey-May comes along.'

'Where will Ryan be?' I asked, apprehensively.

'He's going out too,' she said. 'He's going to watch the rugby. He wants to make this his last big night out too.'

'Well, you'll have to be careful,' I told her. 'And you need to make sure you call me straight away if anything happens.'

I could almost sense her rolling her eyes on the other end of the line.

'OK, Mum,' she said.

'How are you feeling, anyway?'

'Oh, OK. I've been having some stomach pains but they come and go.'

My stomach had tensed as she'd said this. 'Keet, you do know that you could be showing signs of labour?'

'I'll be careful, Mum. I'll stay close and I'll call you if anything happens. OK?'

'OK,' I said, feeling uneasy. 'I'll see you tonight.'

Friday had marked the start of half term and my colleagues had planned a night out to celebrate. Scared Nikitta would give birth early, I'd decided it would be best if I stayed at home. Already I was on tenterhooks and I figured that I wouldn't have been much company, as my eyes would have been glued to my phone all night.

Instead, I came home from work around 4.30pm and made a start on the housework. As I swept the floors and washed the furniture down, I noticed that Missy's hairs were everywhere.

'That bloody dog!' I said to myself.

I'd decided to make a big pot of curry and I was in the kitchen chopping some vegetables when I heard the familiar tap at the window that told me Nikitta and Missy were outside. Predictably, Missy was soon scratching at the door, desperate to get in and devour the tray of chicken she knew I would have bought for her.

As I opened the door, the first thing that struck me was how pretty Nikitta looked. For the last few months she'd looked gaunt and drained but now she was positively glowing. She'd put on some foundation and mascara, which made her gorgeous eyes stand out even more than usual. Even in black leggings and a simple grey cardigan, she'd taken my breath away. Not for the first time, I allowed my eyes to linger on her for a few seconds, wondering how on earth Paul and I had managed to produce such a beautiful girl.

'Wow, Keet!' I said eventually. 'You look absolutely stunning.'

'I always look good, Mum,' she quipped, with a cheeky smile. 'Have you got some chicken for Missy?'

Missy had darted into the kitchen so I followed behind, taking the chicken from the fridge. She lapped it up hungrily.

'How are you now?' I asked Nikitta.

'Oh, fine,' she said dismissively. 'Do you want to see the curtains I've bought for Kelsey-May's room?'

Nikitta had spent the day in the centre of Newport,

shopping with Ryan's mum, Kerry. The curtains were the only things she had left to buy for the nursery. Together, we'd already picked out some gorgeous pink bedding, adorned with the famous 'Me to You' bears, and now she'd chosen the curtains to match.

'Lovely,' I replied, as she handed them to me. 'There's nothing else you need to get now.'

'I can't believe she'll be here in just two more weeks,' Nikitta said.

'Might be sooner than that,' I replied, my eyes fixed on her ever-expanding bump.

At that moment I heard the key turning in the back door, which told me Paul was home. Like Ryan, he was planning to go out to watch the rugby, with his father and a few friends. As is the case in many Welsh towns, rugby is a huge deal in Newport and people are fanatical about it on all sorts of levels, from supporting the local rugby-union club to following the fortunes of the national side. On that fateful Friday, however, it was the biggest match of the year – Wales and England were due to face each other in the annual Six Nations tournament. Needless to say, very few people in the city were planning on staying in.

'Hi, Keet,' Paul called, before disappearing upstairs to have a quick shower. By this point Luke had come downstairs and had instinctively run towards Missy.

'Mum, can Missy stay with us tonight?' he asked, stroking her as he picked her up. Missy always ended up staying at ours whenever Nikitta went out, as no one liked the idea of her being in the flat alone. Truth be told, we all treated her more like a child than a dog. But I knew Kelsey-May's arrival would change everything and we all needed to prepare Missy for the fact that, soon, she wouldn't have our undivided attention.

'Not tonight,' I told him. 'She needs to get used to being in the flat on her own.'

'Please?' Luke protested. 'I don't want her to be in by herself all night.'

'She's not a baby, Luke,' I replied. 'Anyway, I've just cleaned the whole house and it's taken me ages to get her hairs off everything.'

Luke turned to Nikitta. 'Well, can I come and stay with you when you get back in?'

''Course you can,' she said.

Again, I had to put my foot down. I had no objections to Luke staying with Nikitta, as he often did, but as he was only thirteen, I was fairly strict when it came to his bedtime and I liked him to be asleep by 10pm.

'Not tonight, Luke,' I said. 'Keet won't be back until late and you'll be in bed by then.'

'Oh, come on, Mum,' Nikitta chipped in. 'I'll walk round and meet him.'

'The answer's no,' I replied, firmly. As teenagers do, Luke and Nikitta spent a few minutes trying to change my mind before they accepted that I'd made my decision. Nikitta sat on the couch and chatted to me as I prepared the curry in the kitchen. After a while, Paul came downstairs, ready to go out.

'I'm off, Marce,' he called.

'Bye!' I shouted back. 'Have fun.'

'See you later, Keet,' he said, giving Nikitta a kiss and a hug. 'Love you.'

'Bye, Dad,' she replied. 'Love you too.'

A few minutes later Luke came back downstairs.

'Keet, Jenna's car is outside,' he said.

'OK, thanks,' Nikitta replied. She gave me a quick hug and a kiss as she picked up Missy. 'Love you, Mum,' she said. 'I'll see you tomorrow.'

It was the last time I saw my precious daughter alive.

I rubbed my eyes sleepily as I suddenly became aware of the sound of my phone ringing. It sounds awful, but when I saw Ryan's mum's name flash up on my screen, the first emotion I felt was a stab of jealousy. It wasn't yet 8am and I was convinced the only reason she could be phoning was because Nikitta had gone into labour early, as I'd predicted. Nikitta and I were so close and we lived just across the road, while Kerry was a fifteen-minute drive away in Malpas, on the other side of the city. In that split second, I couldn't help but feel a little hurt that she and Ryan had supposedly chosen to phone Kerry first.

'Hello,' I replied, a little woozy but ready to spring into action. Even though he was groggy and hungover, Paul had instinctively jumped out of bed.

'Marcia?' Kerry sounded shakier than I'd expected. 'Is Nikitta there?'

'Here?' I said, confused. 'No, why would she be?'

Kerry inhaled sharply. 'Well, is Ryan there? Did he go out with Paul last night?'

'No,' I said again. 'He went out with his friends. What's going on, Kerry?'

'OK, you better get round there,' she said, her voice wavering with panic. 'I've just had a call from one of the neighbours. The flat's on fire.'

It's hard to explain how it feels to have your world collapse around you, but in that second, it was like someone had ripped my insides out. I didn't have time to respond to Kerry, as my phone fell from my hand onto the bedroom floor. My mother's instinct was screaming that Nikitta and Kelsey-May were in very real danger and that we needed to get to them as soon as possible but it felt like everything was moving in slow motion.

I didn't even try to conceal the terror in my voice. 'Nikitta's flat is on fire!'

I've never seen anyone move so quickly. Paul was already pulling on a pair of jeans and some slippers that were by the bed. He didn't even bother to look for a shirt. I threw on a black T-shirt and some leggings – the first clothes I could find – and we ran downstairs together.

Paul's friend Lloyd had come back to ours for a nightcap after the match and he was asleep on our sofa. Having heard the commotion, he was now sitting bolt upright.

'Nikitta's flat is on fire!' Paul shouted.

I hastily pulled on some boots and we ran out the door.

'Just make sure Luke stays here,' Paul shouted back to Lloyd as we left.

Together, we sprinted towards Nikitta's street. It was a bitingly cold February morning but I could hardly feel the wind on my arms or the drizzle on my face. Under normal circumstances, the journey would take less than two minutes. Today we were running as fast as our legs could carry us but it still seemed like we were on foot for an eternity.

As we rushed through the alleyway leading to the flat, we could already see the blue lights. I felt the blood rush to my head and I could hear my heart pounding but it felt like it was beating in my throat. I could barely stay upright but I knew I had to get to Nikitta. Paul was visibly shaking.

What we were about to see would change our lives forever.

Outside the flat there were two fire engines, two ambulances, several police cars and a huge police van. All of the neighbours were out in the street. The front door had been busted off its hinges. I was met by the stifling smell of smoke and fear coursed through my veins as I realised it was coming from Nikitta's bedroom window. The window was smashed and her white net curtains were blowing into the wind. Kelsey-May's bedroom window was open too but it was obvious where the fire had started.

I slumped onto the pavement. A piercing, feral cry came from my throat as Paul charged towards the house.

'Nikitta!' he screamed, his voice hoarse with terror. 'Nikitta!'

Two firemen had to restrain him as he stood in the garden, screaming our daughter's name over and over, desperate to get inside.

'You can't go in there, sir,' one of the firemen said. 'I'm sorry.'

'What do you mean, I can't go in there?' he shouted. 'My daughter's in there. Let me in!'

Again they had to hold him back. By now his voice had faded to a whimper. He was shivering violently, a combination of panic and the harsh Welsh winter. One of the firemen took his jacket off and silently wrapped it around him.

'Please,' Paul begged. 'Please let me get to my little girl.'

'We don't know if anyone's in there yet, sir,' the fireman told Paul. 'It's not safe for you to go in there. You'll need to stay outside.'

I'm not sure if Paul realised that tears were streaming down his face. In that second, Ryan walked round the corner with Whant and his friend Daniel. As reality began to dawn, I let out another guttural shriek. I tried to push the thought to the back of my mind but, deep down, I knew that if Nikitta wasn't with Ryan, she was in the flat.

Paul made a beeline for our daughter's fiancé, agony etched on his face.

'Where's Nikitta?' he demanded. 'Where is she?'

Ryan's face fell as he took in the scene around him. I didn't take much notice of it at the time but I now realise that Whant's expression barely changed. His black bomber jacket obscured most of his face but he looked entirely unmoved.

'What do you mean?' Ryan said. 'She's in the flat, isn't she?'

Paul is not a violent man but in that second he was so

overcome by anger and frustration that Ryan hadn't been there to protect Nikitta that he punched him square in the face.

'Where the fuck have you been?' he said, sobbing. 'Why is she in there and you're not?'

'Well, I just got home, didn't I?' he said, perplexed. 'What's going on?'

'You just got home?' Paul echoed, his voice shaking with fury. 'You just got home? It's eight o'clock in the morning. How can you have just got home?'

Ryan's mouth fell open, as if he was about to speak, but no words came out.

'How does that work out?' Paul said, but almost to himself this time. 'How can this have happened?'

Ryan didn't offer an explanation and he didn't need to. For now none of that mattered. All we wanted was for someone to tell us it was all a horrible nightmare and that Nikitta was safely tucked up in bed, with Missy by her side.

Denial is a very powerful thing and as the horrific scene began to unfold in front of me, all sorts of alternative scenarios began to formulate in my head. I simply couldn't accept that Nikitta had been in the flat when it had caught fire – my brain wouldn't let me.

A few days beforehand, my Mum had told me a story about how one of her friends had come home to find a group of illegal immigrants squatting in her first-floor flat. The police had come and removed them but half an hour later more returned. They'd got into the flat by climbing up onto the balcony.

In a matter of seconds, I'd convinced myself that the same thing had happened at Nikitta's flat. In my hysterical state, I told myself that there was only one reasonable explanation as to where Nikitta was – she'd stayed at Jenna's and some illegal immigrants had seized the opportunity to break in. If anyone had perished in the flames, it was an intruder. Of course, this would be very sad and the situation wouldn't have been ideal – the flat looked like it had been damaged beyond repair so Nikitta and Kelsey-May would have to move in with us but we'd cope. We'd just have to find a way because they couldn't be gone; they just couldn't.

These thoughts were racing through my head at a hundred miles an hour when Kerry appeared from nowhere. She sat down next to me on the kerb and, without saying a word, put an arm around my shoulder. Of course she meant well but all the grief and terror bubbling up inside of me soon came to the surface and I exploded.

'Why are you here?' I cried, pulling away from her. 'You don't care! You don't even like Nikitta!'

Needless to say, this wasn't true. Kerry was the first person who had spoken to me since we'd arrived on the street and I simply needed someone to scream and shout at. Still, it didn't stop me saying some nasty things to her. Venom was falling out of my mouth but I was clueless as to what I was actually saying. To her credit, she didn't flinch.

'You can say what you like to me,' she said. 'I'm not going anywhere.'

'I don't want you here!' I snapped back, burying my head in my hands.

Eventually, she told me she'd give me some space.

Meanwhile, Paul had run back round to our house to check on Luke. It's impossible to remember the exact order of events but in the chaos Luke soon left and went to Paul's Uncle Patrick's house. Patrick and his wife Cheryl lived a fifteen-minute walk away. In the coming months we would be so grateful to have them on hand.

Paul was soon running back through the alleyway towards the kerb where I was sitting. He made another beeline for the firemen. I was still sat there when I saw he was coming back towards me, his face ashen.

'Marce,' he said quietly. 'I don't know what's happening but I think they might have found someone in there.'

I felt bile rise in my throat but I shook my head furiously. 'No,' I said. 'No, it's not Nikitta. We don't know anything yet. I just know it isn't her, I know it.'

I fixed my gaze defiantly on the flat, still waiting for the firemen to emerge with the body of the intruder I was certain had broken into my daughter's home. Any second now they'd come through the door with the corpse of this nameless, faceless person on a stretcher, their remains covered by a white sheet. We'd bow our heads and say how sad it was, but soon we'd all get back to our own lives. Nikitta would come back from Jenna's and I'd have to break it to her that the home she'd built so lovingly had been destroyed.

Tears glistened in Paul's eyes. 'Let's go home,' he said gently, as they spilled down his cheeks. 'Come on, Marce. I don't think we can do anything here.'

It was only when I tried to stand up that I realised how close to collapse I was. My legs almost buckled beneath me and I felt like I might fall to the ground at any moment. Paul practically carried me back to the house, both of us quietly crying.

I can't say how long it was before there was a knock on the door but it must have been a matter of minutes. Paul answered and my insides twisted as he let two police officers into the living room. They introduced themselves but I'll never remember what their names were. The one who spoke first had a soft, calming voice but I didn't want to hear him speak, as I couldn't bear to listen to the words he was about to say.

'There's no easy way to say this,' he began. I sensed that I was shaking uncontrollably. 'As you are aware, there's been an accident and there has been a fire at your daughter's flat.'

'Where is she?' I cried, grabbing hold of Paul as my legs turned to jelly again.

'I'm afraid firefighters have just recovered a body from the property,' the officer said. 'We have yet to do a formal identification but we believe it is Nikitta.'

I'll never be able to put into words how I felt at that moment. All I can say is that my world seemed to stop, perhaps forever. Finally, my legs gave way. Slowly but surely, I lost control of my body as I sank to the ground. There was an audible thud as I landed awkwardly on my knees but I barely felt any impact as I collided with the cold wooden flooring. I was suddenly aware of the fact that I was struggling for breath as I let out huge, convulsing sobs. No matter how hard I tried, I couldn't seem to get enough air in my lungs.

Paul attempted to pick me up a few times but I was rooted to the spot: a dead weight. Eventually, he collapsed beside me and wrapped his arms around me. It was only then that I realised he was crying as hard – if not harder – than I was. His sobs were deep and throaty, almost animalistic.

'*No*,' we were saying in turn. 'No, no, *no*!'

Neither of us could manage more than one syllable. Besides, it was the only thought in our heads.

No! This can't be happening.

After what seemed like an eternity – but what, in reality, was probably little more than a few minutes – I managed to find my voice. If Nikitta had died in the fire, there was no way Kelsey-May could have survived but there was someone else that hadn't been accounted for. I didn't have the strength to stand up, but between my tears, I somehow got the words out.

'Missy,' I said, choking. 'Have you found Missy?'

'Missy?' the officer asked.

'Missy,' I said again slowly. 'Her pug, she never leaves Nikitta's side.'

'We haven't recovered a body of a dog as far as I know,' he replied. 'But I will make some inquiries.'

I shook my head. 'Wherever Nikitta is, Missy is,' I told him.

The next few minutes passed in a blur of questions. The officers were as gentle as they could be but they had an investigation to conduct and they had to be as thorough as possible.

'Did Nikitta have any tattoos or piercings?' the second officer asked. 'This might help us to identify the body.'

I carefully described all of my daughter's distinguishing features. She had two tattoos – one of Ryan's name on her left wrist and a little scattering of stars stretching from her pelvic bone to her hip. Her ears were pierced in three separate places. The back of her neck was also pierced, as well as her nose and bellybutton.

Paul and I never dreamed that this was anything more than a tragic accident. The second officer kept speaking but it was as if I was underwater, gasping for air, and his voice was a low hum above the surface. I vaguely remember he asked us if Nikitta smoked, or if she liked to light candles, but nothing seemed to make sense.

'She hates smoking,' Paul said. 'She won't even touch an ashtray. She doesn't light candles either.'

Paul looked at me and we both knew exactly what the other was thinking.

'It's her phone!' I said, breaking into another fit of sobs. 'Oh, God, she's slept with her phone.'

'It's never out of her hand,' Paul explained. 'She must have left it charging when she fell asleep.'

Following the initial questions, the officers left us alone for a while so they could make some more inquiries. I was still slumped on the floor when Paul reached for his phone, his hands shaking.

'We should probably let people know,' he said vacantly.

If I'd had the strength, I might have jumped to my feet and ripped the phone from his hands: I didn't want to hear him say Nikitta and Kelsey-May were dead. The more times we said those words, the more real it would become and I felt sure I couldn't take it. But the life had been sucked from me, so all I could do was rock back and forth, sobbing silently, praying I'd soon wake up and discover that this had all been a horrible nightmare.

'Mum?' I heard Paul say. 'Mum, put Dad on!'

There were a few moments of silence as Paul waited for his father to come to the phone. He later told me he couldn't bring himself to tell his mother what had happened, as he knew how much it would destroy her; he didn't have the strength.

'Nikitta's gone,' he finally said. More silence. 'Dad, no, you don't understand, she's gone. There's been a fire. She's gone.'

Paul had broken down again but I couldn't even lift myself from the floor to comfort him. Within minutes, his dad had arrived. Soon, as word spread, relatives and friends began to stream into our living room, their faces white and tear-stained. There must have been around thirty people in the house but I felt a million miles away, as if in some kind of parallel world, like I'd begun to live a life that was never meant for me.

My thoughts turned to Luke. How would he cope with losing his beloved big sister? Of course, they'd had their squabbles but they loved each other so much. How would he ever get over it? How would any of us?

Suddenly, I felt my insides violently lurch as my mind flashed back to the previous evening when Luke had begged me to allow him to stay the night at Nikitta's. I felt two beads of cold sweat form on the back of my neck as I imagined what might have happened if I'd given in. The thought that both of my children could have been in the flat made me feel so ill that I almost had to run to the bathroom to throw up.

I'm not sure how long it was before the police returned but when I heard the knock at the door, my stomach knotted again. This time, there was another officer with them. He was tall and thin, with steely-grey hair and we soon discovered he was Detective Chief Superintendent Geoff Ronayne, the officer Gwent Police had appointed to lead the inquiry. DCS Ronayne was ushered into the living room. Everyone else filed out so he could speak to Paul and me alone.

'Miss Grender,' he said. 'I'm afraid we have found the body of a small dog in Nikitta's bedroom. Could that be Nikitta's dog, Missy?'

I clapped my hands to my mouth as he confirmed what I'd known all along. Somehow, I managed to nod my head, as DCS Ronayne told me that Missy had been found curled up next to Nikitta on the bed. Even in death, they had been inseparable.

I was crying again – those same breathless, convulsing sobs I'd come to know all too well in the coming months. I thought of every time I'd moaned about mopping up Missy's muddy paw prints or sweeping up the hairs that seemed to be permanently strewn across the house. What I'd give now to clean up after her and to hear her scratching at the front door.

I thought about Luke again. He had begged me to let Missy stay at our house while Nikitta was out. If only I'd relented, as I usually did, Missy would have been spared. But I instantly knew that it just wasn't meant to be. How would Missy ever live without Nikitta? Thinking of Nikitta's last moments was tearing me apart. It gave me the smallest crumb of comfort that, perhaps, Missy had been at our daughter's side as she breathed her last, loyal to the end. Paul and I held each for a few moments, crying fresh tears. Now we had yet another loved one to mourn.

'Was it her phone?' Paul eventually croaked. 'Was that what caused the fire?'

DCS Ronayne paused for a few moments and exchanged a glance with his colleague, one of the many officers who visited our house but whose name I can't remember.

'We don't think it was an electrical fire,' he said, choosing his words carefully. 'We've had a look at the plug socket and it's too far from the wall. Nikitta couldn't have been sleeping with her phone on charge.'

'What could it have been?' I demanded. 'How could this have happened?'

'We're exploring all lines of inquiry at the moment,' DCS Ronayne replied.

I shook my head, unable to take anything in. Outside, darkness was falling but I wouldn't notice as one day turned to another and a sleepless, living hell stretched out before us. Any parent who has lost a child will testify that it feels like having part of your soul ripped out and from the moment

Nikitta and Kelsey-May had been discovered in the flat, I knew part of me had died too.

But, as the unanswered questions began to mount, things were about to get much, much worse.

Chapter Six

Evidence

*A*round 8am on the morning of 5 February, just as Paul was begging firemen to let him into Nikitta's burned-out flat as we shivered in the harsh wintry air, Detective Chief Superintendent Geoff Ronayne of Gwent Police received a call on his mobile phone.

He looked at the screen and the name of his deputy, Detective Chief Inspector Steve Mogg, had flashed up. This was nothing unusual, as DCS Ronayne was the on-call senior investigating officer that weekend and often there were incidents that required his attention and expertise. However, he had no inkling that he was about to be called upon to oversee one of the biggest and most complex cases of his career.

There was little time for pleasantries as Detective Chief Inspector Mogg relayed the scene to DCS Ronayne.

Firefighters had been called to a blaze in the Broadmead Park area of Newport. A nineteen-year-old girl, almost nine months pregnant, lay lifeless on her bed among the devastation wreaked by the flames. Needless to say, her unborn but perfectly formed baby girl had died too. Beside her corpse was the body of a small pug dog.

To most people, this would seem like nothing more than a tragic accident but the hairs on DCS Ronayne's neck stood on end.

'OK,' he said slowly. 'She was lying on her back?'

'Yes,' DCI Mogg replied.

'Flat on her back?' DCS Ronayne repeated. His mind was working overtime but he was determined to keep calm. 'She wasn't in the foetal position?'

'No,' DCI Mogg said. 'She wasn't in the foetal position.'

DCS Ronayne took a deep breath. 'I don't think this is a straightforward fire,' he began. 'This could be something more complicated.'

DCI Mogg agreed. Both men had many years of experience in the force and immediately got a sense that something wasn't quite right. They chatted a little more and they both found it strange Nikitta hadn't appeared to make any attempt to defend herself from the flames. Both had witnessed many a tragic scene over the years and they knew that, when someone dies in a fire, they are usually found curled up in a tight ball in an attempt to shield themselves from the blaze.

Firefighters had been called by Nikitta's downstairs neighbour, Sarah Voisey, just before we'd sprinted round to the house. She'd been woken a few hours earlier by a faint beeping sound, which was, of course, the smoke alarm but she'd decided to go back to sleep.

Still, her account confirmed to the police that the alarm was in working order. So why hadn't it woken Nikitta, DCS Ronayne wondered. Even the deepest of sleeps would be disturbed by the persistent beeping of a smoke alarm and Nikitta was likely to be restless anyway as Kelsey-May moved impatiently around her womb.

But even if, against all odds, Nikitta had managed to sleep through the noise and the suffocating heat, Missy would surely have stirred and she would have barked and barked until Nikitta had woken up. DCS Ronayne couldn't understand how anyone, let alone a heavily pregnant woman, could fail to be woken by all of this commotion.

A post-mortem would have been fairly standard in such circumstances but when DCS Ronayne visited us later that day, it was already underway. Nikitta's badly burned remains had been transported to a police mortuary in Cardiff and pathologists were working round the clock to establish the cause of death.

'Don't waste any time,' DCS Ronayne said.

At some point in the confusion the decision was made to arrest Ryan. We're still not quite sure what happened. Feelings were running high after we left the scene and the heavy police presence meant rumours were starting to circulate. He was taken to a nearby station for questioning before DCS Ronayne arrived. Nonetheless, it was important for officers to establish his movements, however unpleasant it might be for the boy.

Ryan was adamant he had a cast-iron alibi. After he'd been at the pub to watch the rugby, he'd gone to a house party. There was someone who could vouch he'd been there all night, he said, until he returned home early the next morning to see the flat ablaze.

To verify this, the officers had to speak to everyone who had been at the party, at an address on Corelli Street, around three miles from Broadmead Park. There was Ryan, of course, and Whant and Daniel, and two girls they'd met when they were out. Ryan insisted no one had left the house until early the next morning, apart from when Whant popped out to borrow some cigarettes from his grandmother sometime after 4am. As usual, he'd left his girlfriend home alone with the kids. Sick of waiting up for him, she'd gone to bed.

DCS Ronayne told officers they needed to build a timeline of Ryan and Nikitta's movements in the twenty-four hours leading up to the fire.

'I promise you I was there all night,' he said. 'Why are you keeping me here like a criminal?'

All of this information was being relayed to DCS Ronayne by the specially trained officers who were probing Ryan on his account of the night. No matter how much they grilled him, he stuck to his version of events.

'I've told you!' he screamed, near breaking point now. 'I was in the flat all night! We all were. None of us left, not one person.' He paused. 'Well, Carl went out to get fags from his nan but he was only gone twenty minutes. He'll tell you, if you don't believe me. I didn't leave. I offered to go with him and he told me not to bother.'

Slowly but surely, DCS Ronayne was beginning to suspect he had a murder on his hands. Often, when someone is murdered, the police start with those closest to the victim and work their way out, so to speak. After all, it's a sad fact that around two women a week are murdered by a current or former partner in the UK.

But DCS Ronayne didn't think this was an open-and-shut domestic-abuse case. Ryan's version of events seemed to add up. Much as I had misgivings about him, I never in a million years dreamt he'd lift a finger to Nikitta. I was in such a state that I don't remember being told he'd been taken to the police station. I'm not even sure I was aware of it, but had I been thinking rationally, I'd have known it didn't make sense.

Staunchly professional, DCS Ronayne didn't betray his fears to us as he sat on our couch asking what appeared to be fairly routine questions. We just assumed he'd come back in a few days to explain how the fire had started and that would be the last of it. We'd be left alone, as months or years of unimaginable grief stretched out before us. It was our worst nightmare; an absolute living hell. How could things get any more awful?

We'd soon find out. As we sat in our crowded living room, lost in tears, the post-mortem was concluded. Pathologists told DCS Ronayne that there was no trace of carbon monoxide in Nikitta's blood.

'This means she couldn't have died in the fire,' DCS Ronayne said instantly. 'She must have died before it started.'

The pathologist then told him they'd found two significant

knife wounds on our beautiful daughter's charred body –
one on her neck and another in her abdomen. She certainly
hadn't died from smoke inhalation: she'd been stabbed.

The wound to Nikitta's neck would have killed her almost
instantly. As far as the pathologist could see, her killer had
then plunged the knife into her stomach.

Into her stomach... DCS Ronayne shuddered at the
thought. Instantly, he sensed he was dealing not just with
murder but with child destruction too. It was a shocking
yet mercifully rare crime, occurring when a foetus deemed
capable of being born alive is deliberately destroyed before
birth.

He knew nothing of us, or of Kelsey-May, but the idea that
someone could deliberately target a poor, defenceless unborn
baby still shocked him to the core; that someone could want
an innocent child dead before they'd even been delivered.

He'd never dealt with anything quite like it before.

'We're dealing with a very dangerous individual here,'
DCS Ronayne told his team.

Time was of the essence. They had to get this person –
whoever they might be – off the street.

Ryan's friends were now being interrogated. By and large,
they stuck to the same version of events as Ryan: they'd
all gone to the pub then back to the house party. The only
person who'd left was Carl Whant, when he'd popped out to
pick up the cigarettes.

'But I'm telling you,' Ryan said. 'He was only gone twenty
minutes, half an hour at most.'

Whant told officers the same thing: he'd left the party to

pick up cigarettes from his grandmother and had returned shortly afterwards. He had been driving a Ford Focus hire car he'd been given through work.

'Look at the CCTV,' DCS Ronayne told his team instinctively. 'Find out everything you can. See if you can track where the car went.'

The officers did pick up a Ford Focus on some CCTV footage. Sure enough, it was spotted in the area where the party had been held around 4am. But it wasn't heading towards Whant's grandmother's house: it was heading for Broadmead Park.

DCS Ronayne had to keep calm. He knew this alone was not enough to raise Whant as a suspect. Immediately he insisted that the vehicle be recovered, alongside the clothes Whant had been wearing on the Saturday evening, and thoroughly examined by the forensics team.

'One more thing,' he said, slowly, as it was far from pleasant. 'I think we need to do some vaginal swabs.'

Thinking of it now makes me want to run to the bathroom and throw up. Deep in the haze of grief, I had no idea this was happening at the time but as it was explained to me later, it made my insides turn over. Hadn't our daughter's killer defiled and demeaned her enough? He'd stabbed her and set her on fire and now her lifeless body was forced to endure this final indignity.

Paul and I were glad DCS Ronayne thought of this though, as it proved to be a vital piece of evidence. While he waited for the results from the laboratory, he asked his team to visit Whant's home. Whant handed over the keys to the car, as well as the jacket and trousers he'd been wearing on the Friday evening, when Nikitta was last seen alive.

'I've never had sex with Nikitta Grender,' he told the officers. 'I did meet up with her once, at a bus stop, but we just had a kiss and a cuddle.'

It was lies, of course. He made Nikitta's skin crawl. She was light years out of his league and he knew it. But it wasn't to be the last odd remark he'd make to the police about her.

He thought he was clever; he was so cocky that he thought he was able to outwit DCS Ronayne and his team but the case against him was mounting. First, the car was swabbed. There didn't appear to be any trace of a crime initially but, on closer inspection, the forensics team discovered three tiny droplets of blood on the underside of the carpet.

As if someone had placed a knife there.

Without hesitation, the blood was analysed: it was Nikitta's.

Then there were the clothes. The officers who'd visited Whant had asked for the light-blue shirt he'd worn on the Friday evening and he claimed he couldn't find it. They were convinced he was lying, so they returned the following evening and searched the house again. The shirt was in the washing machine and they took it away too.

With every moment that passed, there seemed to be a fresh piece of evidence linking Carl Whant to the scene of the crime. Even though the shirt had been washed, it still had traces of Nikitta's blood on the inside. He'd cleaned the outside of his jacket but the lining had made contact with his shirt, so there were tiny traces of blood there too. Of course, there had to be some proof that he had worn the garments. Even though they were in his house, he could easily have claimed he'd borrowed them from a mate and hadn't yet tried them on. But, after hours of painstaking examinations, the team managed to find tiny flakes of his skin on the collars of both the jacket and the shirt.

Whant also had strange scratch marks on his arms, like someone had been trying to fight him off. The police asked him about these but he didn't seem fazed.

'I was in a fight,' he told them, 'with an Asian man.'

He refused to give any more information. But he wasn't savvy enough to know just how much evidence was being collected and how much of it pointed straight to him: he thought he could get out of anything. He'd had brushes with the law before and nothing major had happened, why should this be any different?

The missing piece of the jigsaw, of course, was the vaginal swabs. DCS Ronayne knew that if he could prove Whant had had sex with Nikitta in the hours leading up to her death, they might just have enough evidence to charge him with her murder. There would still be weeks and months of hard graft ahead before they could secure a conviction but it would be a step in the right direction.

Just a few days after Nikitta's body had been found, the results were in. The laboratory phoned DCS Ronayne to give him the findings.

'We've found some semen. There are two profiles,' the lab assistant told him. 'One minor contributor and one major contributor.'

DCS Ronayne inhaled sharply. 'And who do the profiles belong to?' he asked.

'The minor contributor, unsurprisingly, is Ryan Mayes,' the lab assistant said.

DCS Ronayne stayed silent, willing her to go on.

After what seemed like an eternity, she said, 'The major contributor is Carl Whant.'

Chapter Seven
Murder

Neither Paul nor I slept a wink the night we heard the news. Saturday gradually became Sunday, but for us, time had stopped. How could I ever rest again, knowing Nikitta and Kelsey-May were dead? A parent should never have to say goodbye to their child, far less their child and grandchild on the same day.

Instinctively, I closed the door of Nikitta's old bedroom without going inside. It was the room we'd prepared for Kelsey-May – a second nursery so she could spend weekends with us. I couldn't yet bring myself to accept that we'd never use it for that purpose; I wasn't sure I ever would.

A few hours after daylight had crept into our living room, there was a knock at the door: another police officer. A friendly, gentle man in his forties with sandy hair and a

London accent, he introduced himself as Detective Constable Ian Hodgkinson.

'I'm your family liaison officer,' he explained. 'I'm the main point of contact between you and the investigation. If you have any questions, you can ask me.'

At this point, we didn't realise just how significant Ian's appointment was. While family liaison officers (FLOs) can be assigned in lots of different investigations, they are usually deployed in the most serious of cases, particularly when someone has been murdered. On that morning, Ian was just another police officer – one of many who'd filed in and out of our home in the last twenty-four hours. We didn't realise that he would soon become a firm friend. In fact, there would be times throughout the course of the next year when he'd feel like almost part of the family.

We had no idea Ryan had been arrested. All he'd told us was that he'd gone to a party with Daniel, Whant and two female friends after the pub had closed. We had no reason to doubt him and we didn't ask too many more questions. As soon as he was released, he came straight round to the house. I could tell from his face that he was really angry.

'They kept asking me where I was,' he said. 'As if I had something to do with it.'

'Just calm down,' Paul told him. 'At least they've let you go now.'

'My girlfriend and my daughter are dead and the police are treating me like a criminal,' he went on. 'It's not right.'

I'm not sure if the seed of doubt had been sown in my mind at that point but I think I sensed something wasn't right. If the fire had been a tragic accident, why were the police so keen to make sure Ryan had an alibi? However, my grief soon pushed these thoughts to the back of my mind and I assumed it was all part of police procedure.

Shortly after Ryan was released, we got the news we'd been dreading: the body that had been found in the flat was formally identified as Nikitta's. Normally, a family member would have been asked to identify her remains but she'd been so badly burned that this wasn't possible. Instead, the police had used the information I had given them about her tattoos and piercings and they were satisfied that it was our daughter they'd recovered from the flames. Of course, this only confirmed what we'd known all along but it didn't make it any easier to deal with.

Gradually, friends and neighbours began to knock on the door to offer their condolences. Some brought flowers and we appreciated every single gesture. Many didn't know what to say, so they just gave us a supportive hug and left it at that.

Soon, the house was like a florist's. We kept all of the wreaths on a table in the living room and there were more with every hour that passed. We were so broken that we could barely leave the house, so family and friends brought us shopping and cooked us meals, coaxing us to eat even though it was the last thing on our minds.

Three days after the fire, we were sitting in the living room with some family when there was yet another knock on the back door. Paul answered and from the couch, I could see Carl Whant standing on the doorstep in the same black jacket he'd been wearing on the morning of the fire.

A chill shot through me as I surveyed him from a distance. In his hand was a bunch of cheap flowers bought from a petrol station.

'I just wanted to say I'm sorry about Nikitta,' he told Paul as he opened the door. 'I wanted to give you these.'

He handed over the flowers and Paul accepted them. 'OK, thanks very much,' he replied.

As I've already mentioned, Whant had a bad stammer and it often took him a while to get his words out, but that day his voice seemed louder and clearer than usual.

'If there's anything I can do, you know where I am,' he said. 'Give us a cwtch.'

Cwtch is Welsh for a cuddle and I felt the colour drain from my face as he pulled Paul into a hug.

'Marce, you've gone white,' my uncle – also called Paul – said.

'I don't want him here,' I replied. I realised I was shaking. 'I don't want him in my house, make sure he doesn't come in.'

'What's wrong?' Uncle Paul said, laying his hand on my arm. 'Come on, Marce. Loads of people have been coming and going. The lad obviously just wants to pay his respects.'

But I was adamant. 'No,' I said. 'Nikitta didn't like him, he's not welcome.'

'I'll go and tell Paul you don't want any visitors,' Uncle Paul said, but Paul was already walking back into the living room, clutching the flowers.

'Get those out of the house!' I said, rising from my chair.

'Oh, come on, Marce, don't be horrible,' Paul replied.

'He's just come round to pay his respects, like everyone else.'

'I don't want those flowers in my house,' I repeated, my voice trembling. 'Nikitta didn't like him, you know that.'

'He's taken the time to get some flowers and bring them round,' Paul insisted. 'I think we should put them on the table with the others.'

Drained, I simply didn't have the energy to argue. 'Fine,' I said. 'Do what you want with them then.'

I can't explain why Whant made me feel so uneasy that night, but for the rest of the evening, I was seething. Every few seconds my eyes would be drawn to his flowers on the table. They looked so out of place next to those from genuine well-wishers, many of whom had known and loved Nikitta for a long time. It just didn't feel right.

It was fortunate at the time neither Paul nor I had an inkling this was fast becoming a murder inquiry and that Whant was the prime suspect. If we'd known what we do now, we might have killed him there and then with our bare hands.

In the coming days, friends and family would ask if me if I'd had some kind of mother's intuition; a sort of sixth sense that he'd been responsible for Nikitta and Kelsey-May's deaths. It would be easy to convince myself this was the case but looking at things rationally, I don't think I suspected he'd had anything to do with the fire at that stage.

Put simply, he'd always given me the creeps. I knew he'd perved over private pictures on Nikitta's phone and that he often made comments that made her uncomfortable. He had never respected her while she was alive, so it made me angry that he was pretending to be respectful now she was dead. I also knew he was a bad influence on Ryan. I didn't doubt that he had pestered Ryan to go out on the night my daughter had died, leaving her alone in the flat. I suppose I blamed him in some way but even then, I don't think I sensed the evil he was capable of.

It wasn't until the next day that we discovered the awful truth about Nikitta and Kelsey-May's deaths. Much later, we were told that when Whant had come to our house to offer his condolences, the police had already questioned him in connection with the fire. Forensic teams had swabbed his car and found our daughter's blood on the underside of the floor carpet. Time was running out for Whant and he had to do something – anything – to persuade us he was innocent.

The knock at the door came in the morning. I'd managed to drag myself into the shower, though even washing felt like a tremendous effort. I was coming downstairs when I caught sight of DCS Ronayne on the front doorstep.

'It's the guy from Saturday again,' I said to Paul. 'Why is he here?'

Mentally drained, I couldn't face any more seemingly pointless questions about candles or ashtrays much as I appreciated DCS Ronayne had a job to do.

'I think something's up,' Paul replied. 'Why else would they come back?'

As far as I was concerned, it couldn't get any worse:

Nikitta was never coming home and we'd never meet our first grandchild. What could he possibly say that could hurt us any more?

Paul let him in and they exchanged some pleasantries but it was obvious there was little time for preamble.

'I think you should sit down,' he told us both. 'There has been a significant development in the inquiry.'

'Do they know what caused the fire?' I asked, too apprehensive to take a seat.

DCS Ronayne paused for what seemed like an eternity. 'We don't think this was an accident,' he finally said.

Paul and I looked at each other, incredulous.

'What?' we said, almost in unison.

'I'm sorry to be the one to have to tell you this,' DCS Ronayne continued, 'but we have reason to believe the fire was started on purpose. We think Nikitta was murdered.'

The next thing I knew, I was losing control of my body again. I felt myself sway and Paul tried his best to hold onto me but I slid through his hands and dropped to my knees, just like I'd done a few days earlier when I'd been told Nikitta and Kelsey-May were dead.

Murder.

The word was going round and round in my head but I couldn't quite wrap my brain around the idea that someone had wanted my daughter and granddaughter to die. Murders happened on crime dramas, or to people on the news, not to normal families like ours. Paul knelt down beside me and tried to comfort me but I was hyperventilating, struggling for air again, feeling like I might die too.

'How do you know this?' I finally asked. 'How do you know this is what happened?'

DCS Ronayne bowed his head. 'We can't say too much at this stage,' he said. 'But the post-mortem revealed some wounding to Nikitta's body. We believe her injuries are consistent with those of a murder victim.'

Nausea washed over me as I imagined a stranger breaking into Nikitta's flat in the dead of night and killing her in cold blood. Who could have done this? How did they get in? I could feel my body shuddering violently as I thought of her last moments, of how terrified she would have been and how she'd have tried to protect Kelsey-May. Was she screaming for Paul and me? Was it quick, or did she suffer?

'Tell me what happened,' I croaked. 'Tell me what happened to my daughter.'

DCS Ronayne told us he couldn't explain any more as the investigation was at such a critical stage. In retrospect, I'm glad he was so professional. Had he or any of his officers divulged crucial information to us at this point, we might not have got justice for Nikitta and Kelsey-May as their killer's lawyers could have argued that he hadn't had a fair trial.

But on that awful day that was the last thing on my mind. I needed to know exactly what my baby had gone through. What were the wounds that DCS Ronayne had spoken of? Had these been caused by the fire, or had this animal done something else to her? Of course, he couldn't go into detail and there were far more questions than answers.

'We need to establish if Ryan or Nikitta had any enemies,' DCS Ronayne went on. 'Is there anyone who comes to mind?'

Paul's head was in his hands. 'You think this was someone they knew?' he eventually said, looking up.

'We're exploring all possible lines of inquiry,' DCS Ronayne said. 'Has Ryan had any arguments with anyone?'

We looked at each other, bewildered.

'Not that we know of,' I said, though in truth, I had no idea.

'You don't know if he owed any money to anyone?' DCS Ronayne said. 'Was he involved with loan sharks?'

Again, we didn't have a clue. Nikitta knew that we'd had reservations about her relationship with Ryan and although we were on good terms now, she was highly unlikely to tell us if he'd done anything we'd disapprove of.

'Who could have done this?' Paul kept saying, over and over. 'Who?'

Dozens of names swirled around our heads. Of course, Nikitta had had the odd squabble with her friends but she had no real enemies – certainly no one who'd feel strongly enough to kill her. We were going crazy, mentioning anyone and everyone we could think of, casting our minds back to all sorts of silly playground disputes. Nothing made any sense.

'You have to find the bastard who did this to my daughter,' Paul said to DCS Ronayne. 'Or I'll find him myself.'

'We're doing all we can,' he replied.

'Well, I hope you find him soon,' I said, weeping. 'Because God help him if we get to him before you do.'

Later that day our family liaison officer, Ian Hodgkinson, paid us a visit. He explained as much as he could about what the officers knew and tried to reassure us that the police were doing all they could but we'd been plunged into a fresh agony and were barely able to concentrate.

Family and friends were still staying with us round the clock and we must have told them what had happened but I can't remember the conversations. I suspect they were so painful that I've simply blocked them out. For the rest of the day I just stared into space, unable to emerge from my zombie-like trance. Just a few days earlier I'd been a normal mum with a normal life, excited for the birth of my first grandchild. Now my life would never be normal again.

That night, Paul and I held each other and cried as another sleepless night turned into day.

Soon there was another knock on the door from DCS Ronayne. Neither of us had dared switch on the television or pick up a newspaper but if we had, we'd have been shocked to find that Nikitta's death was making headlines all over the UK.

When DCS Ronayne told us to ask our family and friends to leave the house, we knew he had important news. Luke was at home and we had to send him to his room. I understood that he was too young to listen to such a gruesome conversation but it broke my heart to think of him upstairs, alone. Our family and friends – particularly Paul's Uncle Patrick and his wife Cheryl – had done a fantastic job of looking after him since the fire, making sure he kept up his strength and giving him a shoulder to cry on, but no one could take his pain away. As a mum, I've never felt more helpless, or more guilty: I wanted so badly to make it all better, but I never would be able to.

When DCS Ronayne explained that detectives had made an arrest, I braced myself for the name that was about to pass his lips. I expected it would be someone I'd never met before – an opportunistic psychopath who had chanced upon Nikitta's flat and decided to do the unthinkable – because the idea that we could have come face-to-face with her killer seemed ludicrous.

'I wanted to let you know before any information is released to the media,' he said. 'The person we have arrested is Carl Whant.'

'Carl Whant?' I echoed blankly. 'Carl Whant, Ryan's cousin?'

'I'm afraid so,' DCS Ronayne replied. 'He hasn't been charged as yet but he is in custody at the moment.'

I looked at Paul and suddenly our eyes were drawn to the table, where Whant's flowers still sat.

'That bastard!' he shouted. 'That fucking bastard!'

It was incomprehensible. As much as Nikitta had disapproved of him, Whant was like a brother to Ryan. Kelsey-May was his flesh and blood.

'But he came round here the other day,' I said, my voice trembling. 'He came round here with flowers.'

Paul's face was contorted with rage. I've never seen such pain in his eyes and my insides twisted sharply as it suddenly occurred to me that my lovely partner had unwittingly hugged his daughter's killer.

'Bastard!' he said. 'Bastard! I gave him a cwtch! I gave him a fucking cwtch!'

'You weren't to know,' I said softly, tears spilling down my face. 'Think of how many people you cwtched…'

'I gave him a fucking cwtch!' Paul turned to DCS Ronayne. 'He came to our door with flowers and he gave me a hug. What kind of fucking monster does that?'

I asked DCS Ronayne how they knew it was Whant but all he could tell me was that they had strong forensic evidence linking him to the scene of the crime. We had no choice but to take his word for it and after he left, we collapsed on the couch, moving between uncontrollable tears and fits of violent rage.

'You were right, Marce,' said Paul with a choked sob. 'You were right. I can't believe I let him touch me.'

'I didn't want him here but I never thought he could have done this,' I said, sobbing. 'Not to his own family.'

Suddenly, Paul's expression shifted and I saw genuine hatred in his eyes. 'I could have killed him,' he said. 'When he was here the other night, I could have fucking killed him. I had the chance and I missed it. I could have fucking had him! Marce, what if he gets away with this?'

'I wish you had killed him,' I said. 'If he ever comes round here again, I'll make sure someone does.'

Soon we were interrupted by a knock at the back door: it was Ryan. His face was deathly white, as if he'd just seen a ghost. I knew instantly that the police had called to tell him of the development, too.

'It can't be true,' he said. 'It's not Carl.'

Paul and I looked at each other.

'Ryan—' I began.

'He was with me all night,' he went on, as if he hadn't heard me. 'It can't have been him.'

Inside I was consumed with rage. I wanted to smack

Ryan hard across the face. He'd brought this monster into Nikitta's life and then left her alone in the flat so Whant could kill her and the child she'd so looked forward to having. Now here he was in my house, defending him, protesting his innocence. I needed someone to blame and God, did I blame Ryan. In that second, I wished I'd never set eyes on him.

But I didn't hit him. I didn't lash out, or scream, or swear. Instead I took a deep breath and bit my lip so hard, I tasted blood. With as much composure as I could muster, I thought of Nikitta: what would she have wanted me to do?

It was a no-brainer. She had loved Ryan – he was her fiancé and Kelsey-May's father. She'd have wanted us to look after him.

'Come into the living room,' I told him. 'You need to sit down.'

'The police have a lot of evidence,' Paul said. 'I'm sorry, Ryan. But I think he did it.'

As gently as we could, Paul and I tried to coax him out of his state of denial but we knew it would be a few days before he'd accept that Whant was the killer. It was the ultimate betrayal, after all.

It wasn't long before our family and friends returned. Tearfully, we passed on the news. Disbelief was etched on everyone's faces as we told them who it was.

'He had the audacity to come round here with flowers?' my Dad said. 'Knowing he'd done this to Nikitta?'

One of my Dad's friends – a colourful character named Twinny – had come round with him and my Mum.

'Where are they?' he said. 'Marce, show me the flowers. I'll take care of them for you.'

I pointed out the cheap bunch of petrol-station flowers on the table. In the chaos, I'd forgotten to throw them out but now their very presence was taunting me.

Twinny seized the flowers in his hands. He threw open the back door and, one by one, ripped their heads off. A sea of pink, purple and yellow petals cascaded through the air and he stamped on each one as it fell to the ground. He didn't miss a single bud. When only the stems were left, he ran across the garden to the woods at the back of our house. Without saying a word, he began thrashing the remains of the bouquet against a tree.

Chapter Eight

Kelsey-May

A few days later we were told that Carl Whant had been charged with Nikitta's murder. We learned he'd also been charged with rape and child destruction. I can't remember much about the conversation, or who told me. I just remember collapsing again, my body hitting the hard living-room floor as the room slid out of focus. We didn't yet know about the vaginal swabs, or the wounds to Nikitta's stomach. Ian Hodgkinson explained later that they had some sort of forensic evidence but said he couldn't go into detail.

Not that we could have processed any detail. It was hard enough trying to get our heads around the fact that Nikitta, Kelsey-May and Missy were gone.

'How could anyone do that?' I croaked. 'How *could* they? To anyone, never mind a heavily-pregnant nineteen-year-old girl?'

I was so consumed in my own pain that I barely noticed how much it was ripping Paul apart. What such a revelation must be like for a father, I don't know.

'She would have been shouting for me,' he said through his sobs. 'I know it, she would have been screaming for her Dad. That's why he did what he did, Marce. He knew she'd tell me and God knows what I'd have done then. That's why he did it.'

We sat on the sofa, wrapped in each other's arms, staring into the distance. We'd lost all concept of time. Without Nikitta and Missy, minutes seemed like hours and hours felt like days. But, at other times, I'd be in such a daze that I hadn't noticed time passing at all.

It might sound strange but I also missed Kelsey-May desperately. Even though she hadn't yet been born, already she was part of the family. She had a name, clothes, toys and two nurseries – a proper identity. She belonged here with us. I ached to hold her in my arms, to stroke her little head, to soothe her and sing to her. Tears spilled down my cheeks as I thought of the songs I'd hummed to Nikitta when she was a little girl. I'd so looked forward to teaching them to Kelsey-May. How could anyone with a shred of humanity in their body have put us through this torture?

'When can I see them?' was all I could ask. 'When can I see my babies?'

'Soon,' Ian promised. 'As soon as I can, I'll take you to them.'

'Why can't we see them now?' Paul asked hoarsely.

Ian took a deep breath. Slowly, he tried to explain as best

he could that they had to ensure DCS Ronayne and his team had got absolutely everything they needed from the post-mortem before we could see Nikitta, or else we might risk contaminating some key evidence.

At this stage he couldn't tell us anything about what kind of evidence they had, or how they'd managed to connect Whant to the scene of the crime – only that the evidence they had was already compelling. My mind was already beginning to work overtime and I begged him for answers: I just needed to know something, however painful it might be.

'I'm afraid I can't tell you any more than that, Marcia,' he said gently. 'This is going to be hard to swallow but we need to make sure he gets a fair trial.'

A fair trial? If I hadn't been sitting down, I might have fallen to the ground again in shock. It seemed ludicrous that we should be thinking of his rights at a time like this and at first, I went off my head. But the more Ian spoke about the court process, the more I began to realise he had a point: the jury had to be convinced beyond reasonable doubt that Whant had killed Nikitta. All his defence lawyers had to do was plant a seed of doubt in their minds, or worse still, try to get him off on a technicality. If the police were seen to be sharing confidential evidence before it was revealed in court, it could be enough to have the case thrown out completely. It was galling but we just had to accept it.

For the next few days I lurched between violent rage and crushing despair, often finding myself caught in the middle. Our house was usually full of visitors; family and friends urging us to try to eat and sleep. I'm not sure how we could have functioned without them, as they quietly made meals and went grocery shopping. I think at one point my kettle packed in because they'd made so many cups of tea for all of the visitors.

Patrick and Cheryl were absolute godsends, especially in those first few days. Without them, I'm genuinely not sure how we, or Luke, would have coped. When Ian or any of the other officers were giving us information about the case, he had to go upstairs to his room. It broke my heart to think of him sitting all on his own, even just for ten minutes, not least because I was sure he'd be able to hear what was being said and no child should ever have to hear about anything so distressing, especially when it involves his own sister. After a few days, Patrick and Cheryl began to take Luke away when the police came round, or whenever they felt he needed some space. Our family home, once so happy, was now like a pressure cooker. It was only a matter of time before someone burst into tears, unable to cope with the reality of the situation.

We never asked Patrick and Cheryl to do this – they just acted on instinct and never asked for any thanks. We'll always be so grateful to them for their support.

After what seemed like an eternity, Ian told us we could go to the police mortuary to see Nikitta and Kelsey-May. It had only been ten days since the fire but it had felt like a lifetime. We felt we ought to give Luke the chance to come with us but we weren't surprised when he opted to stay at Patrick and Cheryl's. What thirteen-year-old could cope with what we were about to see? We could barely comprehend it ourselves.

Ian explained that we would be able to hold Kelsey-May but that she, too, had some wounds on her body. He couldn't tell us where and that made my head spin. What had this monster done to her?

We travelled to Cardiff in a police car with our parents. Ryan, who was still slipping in and out of denial, had been given his own family liaison officer: a lovely young guy called Paul, who would take him and Kerry to the mortuary in a separate car.

Newport is only fifteen miles from Cardiff and normally the journey is over before you know it, but as we whizzed along the motorway on that cold February night, I never wanted to arrive there. I thought about Nikitta's body and what state it might be in. Would I ever be able to get those images out of my head? I thought about all of my precious memories of my beautiful girl and what this last image of her might be. Would I ever recover?

No one really spoke at all on the way there. Lost in thought, I was looking out of the window. I wasn't crying, though; I was just a bit numb. I'd managed to put up a bit of a barrier, even with those closest to me. Mum and Dad were trying to be strong but Nikitta had been their pride and joy. This was tearing them apart too. If I broke down, I was sure they would be next, and I couldn't cope with their tears. Not yet.

Paul's parents weren't faring any better. Their heads were fixed on the ground, their faces ashen. When we pulled into the car park, I stayed rooted to my seat for a second. What would happen, I wondered, if we just turned back and pretended this wasn't real? Couldn't we just go home? Surely then we'd all realise it was a big mistake. It wasn't Nikitta in there, after all, Ian would say. We got it wrong. Then I'd hear Missy pawing at the front door. I'd open it and Nikitta would give me a hug, bump even bigger than before, as her precious pug bounded into the living room, leaving a trail of hair and destruction in her wake.

I still couldn't accept that this would never happen again. But on that day the stark reality of the situation was staring me in the face. The moment I saw my daughter and granddaughter on those cold mortuary slabs was the moment it all became real. The moment I couldn't live in denial any longer.

There were some sofas outside the room where Nikitta and Kelsey-May were being held and we were told to sit down before we went in.

It sounds crazy but in that instant, I felt sorry for Ian. I'd been so aware of my own agony that it didn't occur to me how this must have felt for him. He was a police officer, sure, and he'd probably seen some nasty sights in his time but few cases were as gruesome as this. And it was easy to forget he was a person too, with his own family. How must it have felt for him, spending every day with us, being the one to break all the awful news to us, one hammer blow after another?

Standing outside the mortuary, I saw the pain etched on his face for the first time. I could tell he was trying so hard to conceal it but I just knew it was there.

He bowed his head and cleared his throat. 'OK,' he said

slowly. 'When you go in, Nikitta's body will be covered by a cloth.' He paused. 'I can't tell you what to do but...' he took a deep breath. 'I would strongly advise you not to look.'

I think I'd fallen into Paul's arms as he said this but I can't be sure.

'What has he done to her?' Paul croaked. 'What could be so bad, that...?' his voice tailed off as images of Nikitta's badly-burnt body flashed through his mind.

'It's up to you,' Ian said. 'But, if I were you... I can't make the decision for you, but I think I'd want to remember her as she was.'

Paul and I didn't say anything but we silently decided to take his advice. In life, Nikitta had been so beautiful – everyone had commented on how gorgeous she was. When I closed my eyes, I could still see her stunning face as clear as day. We didn't want our precious memories to be tainted.

I went in first. As Ian had told us, Nikitta's body was lying on a mortuary slab, covered by a purple velvet sheet. There was a Moses basket next to her, where they'd put little Kelsey-May.

The grief hit me like a tidal wave. I wasn't aware of anything, or anyone, around me apart from Nikitta and Kelsey-May. I couldn't decide who to go to first – my daughter or my granddaughter. It was an agonising choice. For a moment, I stood in the centre of the room, tortured by the dilemma.

In the end, I ran to Kelsey-May and took her to Nikitta. I knew that's what Nikitta would have wanted. It was only then that my legs gave way and I slumped down next to my daughter's body, hugging them both and crying so hard, I thought I might die too. How could this be happening?

Through the cloth, I touched my daughter's perfect face. I thought of the way she'd looked the last time I'd seen her: of the care she'd taken over her foundation and mascara; how lovely she'd looked. For the first time in her pregnancy, she hadn't looked worn out but truly glowing. I tried my hardest not to think about what Whant had done to her; what horrors lay beneath the smooth velvet sheet but it was so, so hard.

This would have been no quick, painless death. I felt beads of sweat forming on my forehead as thoughts of her last moments began to torment me. Of course, we didn't know exactly what had happened to her but in a way that was worse as thousands of horrendous scenarios flashed through my mind. Nikitta had never liked Whant but Ryan had loved him like a brother. He'd trusted him. Yet he'd broken into their home in the dead of night and violated his girlfriend in the most disgusting way imaginable, before killing her and their unborn child.

It was then that I took my first good look at Kelsey-May. I'd been holding her to me, in a state of collapse, but I hadn't had time to take in her little features. All we could see was her face, her hands and feet. I'd imagined she'd look exactly like Nikitta as a newborn baby but she was completely different. She had Ryan's nose and his eyes, and the Brunnock hands – long, thin fingers, just like her Grancha. She was so perfect and her features seemed so peaceful. It was hard to believe she was dead.

As I rocked her in my arms, I was almost blinded by my tears. I thought I might stay on the cold hard floor forever, just holding her and pretending all of this wasn't real. Cradling your first grandchild should be such a special moment, no one expects it to happen in a police mortuary.

After a few minutes, the room slowly came into focus again. Paul was by Nikitta's body, kissing her cheek through the cloth.

'I love you,' he said through his tears. 'I love you.'

He was saying it over and over again, as if it might bring her back if he kept saying the words out loud. It was only then that I became aware of the horrible white hat they'd put on Kelsey-May's head. It was faded and dirty, like a really old hand-me-down. She was wearing a dreadful white coat and dress too. The clothes looked really old and ugly. My grief momentarily gave way to anger as I imagined how Nikitta's face would look if she caught sight of her baby in those awful old things. She was so fashion-conscious and we'd lovingly picked out so many beautiful outfits for Kelsey-May, she couldn't be laid to rest as she was – she just couldn't.

Instinctively, I went to remove her hat but the mortuary nurse – a lovely woman called Claire – stopped me just in time.

'I'm so sorry,' she said gently. 'You'll have to keep her hat on.'

'But it's horrible!' I said. 'Would you want your baby wearing this? Nikitta wouldn't have it – she just wouldn't. Please let me take it off!'

Claire touched my arm supportively. 'I am so sorry,' she said again, 'but I just can't let you take it off.'

My heart almost stopped as I realised why I wasn't allowed to remove it. I remembered what Ian had said about the wounding to Kelsey-May's body. What had he done to her? How much more could we take?

I didn't want to let go of Kelsey-May. As selfish as it sounds, I didn't even want Ryan to take her from me. I touched her cold lips and kissed her freezing little cheeks, drinking in every last detail of her, just as I had with Nikitta on the day she was born. But I knew I couldn't keep her to myself forever. Eventually, I turned to Paul. He was still by Nikitta's side, clinging to the cloth, with his head in his hands.

'Would you like to hold her?' I asked, softly.

Anxiety flashed across Paul's face. Despite coming from a big family, he's always been a bit nervous around tiny babies, scared to pick them up in case he holds them in the wrong way or hurts them somehow. As strange as it may sound, I knew instinctively that's what was going through his head. Of course, he couldn't hurt Kelsey-May because she was already dead but neither of us could think of her like that. It was just like she was sleeping peacefully in my arms.

Paul's mum stepped forward. Her face was white and her eyes bloodshot but she was calmer than the rest of us at that moment. She laid her hand on his arm.

'Let me take her, Marce,' she said. 'Please.'

I passed Kelsey-May to her and I felt like my heart was

being slowly and painfully ripped out. My steely facade had slipped and now my sobs were laid bare for all to see. It was one of the few times I've ever let my mask slip.

As Paul's mum cradled her great-granddaughter, a single tear rolled down her cheek. I suddenly became aware of the noise around me. Everyone was in tears: Paul, me, Ryan, Kerry and our parents.

I turned to look at the back of the room and the FLOs – Ryan's and ours – were standing with their heads bowed. They were big, tough blokes used to dealing with unspeakable acts of violence and the families left to pick up the pieces.

They were both crying too.

It sounds ridiculous but for a second I was overwhelmed by a huge sense of pity for them. Paul, Ryan's FLO, was a bit younger than Ian and seeing him standing there, trying to stifle his tears, just broke me. They were police officers, sure, but they were people too. They hadn't asked for this to happen either. They had families to go home to; loved ones of their own. No doubt they were putting themselves in our shoes and it was tearing them apart.

They looked so uncomfortable. I know that if they'd had the choice, the FLOs would have left us to it and let us see the girls in private. But their bodies were still being held as evidence and we couldn't be left alone with them. We had to do everything in our power to make sure Whant's defence didn't have a leg to stand on; that there was no way they could argue his case hadn't been handled properly. It was the most surreal of situations.

Paul's mum was still holding Kelsey-May when I turned

back round. Paul was standing next to her, looking at our granddaughter, crying softly. He looked like he was in a trance; an almost dreamlike state.

'Would you like to hold her?' his mum asked quietly. 'Paul?'

'No,' he said, shaking his head, as if he'd come back to reality. 'No, it doesn't feel right. I'll hold her in the wrong way.'

'Paul,' his mum said slowly. 'I think you should. This is the only chance you'll have. She's your granddaughter. You'll regret it if you don't, I know you will.'

Paul looked to me, torn. 'It doesn't feel right. I can hold her but Nikitta can't.'

'Hold her, Paul,' I choked. 'You'll wish you had if you don't.'

I watched as Paul's mum passed our little granddaughter to him. He took her in his arms, a little awkwardly at first, but then he relaxed. He took her tiny hand in his and kissed it.

'She's perfect, Marce,' he said through his tears. 'She's just perfect.'

'I know,' I replied. 'I know.'

Holding our granddaughter for the first time should have been one of the proudest and happiest moments of our lives but we were distraught as we tried to contemplate all of the milestones Kelsey-May would miss. Nikitta wouldn't phone us excitedly to tell us that she'd said her first word, or rush round, beaming with pride, when Kelsey-May took her first steps. She wouldn't start school, or go to her friends' birthday parties. She would be frozen in time, forever a baby, nothing more than a memory.

Paul passed Kelsey-May to Ryan. He took her in his arms and kissed her lips.

'Daddy loves you,' he said as he cried. I had to turn away – I couldn't deal with his pain on top of my own. I still blamed him for bringing Whant into Nikitta's life and leaving her alone the night she died, though I'd vowed to stand by him because I knew Nikitta would have wanted that.

I wondered if I should go to him. Should I try to console him, I thought, as I watched him cling to his dead daughter, crying for the baby he'd never know. I knew Nikitta would have liked that but I just couldn't: it was too much. I could barely keep upright.

Besides, his own mother was there. It was her place to comfort him. She soothed him as he cuddled Kelsey-May before taking her in her own arms.

Too soon it was time to go. I begged to hold Kelsey-May one last time before Claire took her and put her back in her Moses basket. Like the clothes, the basket was ugly too, with a tatty old blue sheet laid inside. It seemed so unfair when we had a beautiful pink-and-white Moses basket at home waiting for her – one Nikitta had chosen so carefully.

'Please tell me I can come back,' I said to Claire. 'Please let me get her some new clothes. She can't wear those. Nikitta would have a fit.'

I knew it wasn't Claire's fault that the clothes were so ugly and old. The mortuary obviously had a tight budget and it wasn't within her control. But we couldn't lay Kelsey-May to rest in those horrible things.

Claire smiled and squeezed my hands. I saw the tears glisten in her eyes too.

'Of course you can come back,' she said. She scribbled on a piece of paper and handed it to me. 'Here is my mobile number. Call any time of the day or night. Even if it's two o'clock in the morning, I'll come and open up for you.'

I was so overwhelmed by her kindness that I didn't know what to say. In the end, I couldn't find the words to say anything.

The next day brought with it another fresh agony – that of having to choose an outfit for Kelsey-May to make her final journey in. We hadn't yet had word of when the bodies might be released to us for a funeral but there was no way I was going to have my granddaughter dressed in anything but the best.

I knew I'd have to go into town to choose some clothes and that in itself was a huge ordeal. Slowly but surely we'd started to become aware of the huge press interest in the story. We'd had a few reporters knocking on the door but we'd politely but firmly told them we didn't have anything to say. More than anything, we were petrified we'd say too much and do something to prejudice the trial. We didn't know anything about the laws surrounding newspapers and court cases and we were terrified they'd print something that would get us into trouble and harm our case.

Word had slowly started to filter back to us that there were loads of reporters camped outside Nikitta's flat – not just from the newspapers but from the TV channels too. They were filming people coming round to leave tributes: flowers for Nikitta and teddies for Kelsey-May. From that moment on, the TV in our house was turned off. We didn't switch it back on for months; we couldn't bear to see our daughter's beautiful face flash up on the screen, happy and so full of life. It would have been just too painful.

Thankfully, none of the cameras caught me leaving the house, as they were all round at Nikitta's. Still, it didn't make it any easier walking around, as I was sure everyone was staring at me. Newport might be a city but it's a relatively small one and things like this don't happen very often. You'd be surprised at how many people know each other and I knew Nikitta's murder was the talk of the town.

There was only one place I wanted to go for Kelsey-May's outfit: a lovely little boutique called Marina's. It had opened when Nikitta was a toddler and the clothes were always so beautiful. They were quite expensive, so I could rarely afford to buy a dress from there but anytime I did, she looked so beautiful. Paul's mum agreed to come along with me. I think she was scared I would collapse under the weight of my grief if I went alone.

As I walked along the street, I kept my head down, wishing I could blend into the background and become invisible. I wasn't sure if people were looking at me or not, but what struck me most was how normal everything seemed. Harassed mums pushed buggies and shouted at their children not to run into the road and shoppers strained under the weight of their grocery bags as they waited at the bus stop.

I wanted to scream at them. How could they go about their business as normal, like nothing had happened? How could the world just keep turning without Nikitta in it? Why was life just allowed to go on? I must have passed dozens of people on my way to the shop – just a tiny fraction of the hundreds of thousands of people who lived in Newport and the surrounding area.

All I could think was: why me? Why my family? Out of all these people, why had it happened to us?

As I pushed open the door of the boutique, I had to bite my lip really hard to stop the tears from flowing.

The clothes were all so beautiful but I had to be mindful of how much they cost. It wasn't like picking up a cheap dress in the supermarket – they were pretty pricey. Of course, I wanted nothing but the best for Kelsey-May but we had a funeral to pay for too and money doesn't grow on trees.

I had my heart set on a gorgeous pink-and-white lace dress. As I picked it up and looked at the price tag, my heart sank. It wasn't within my budget; it wasn't even close. A tear snuck down my cheek as I pictured Kelsey-May wearing it, thinking of how beautiful she'd look. Paul's mum placed a supportive hand on my arm but she couldn't say anything to comfort me. What use were words in a time like this?

It was only as I placed the dress back on the rail that I became aware of the owner standing behind me. He was an older man, from India, and I recognised him instantly because I'd been into the shop so many times.

'I hope you don't mind me saying this,' he said. 'But I realise who you are.'

I didn't know what to say, so I just stared at him blankly. I prayed he wouldn't ask me any questions, as I wasn't sure I could cope.

But he went on, 'You choose anything you want. You can have it. Please. We will take care of it.'

I was aware that the tears had begun to flow, thick and fast, but still no words would come. I picked up the dress again and held it in my hands, delicately fingering the fabric.

'Choose what you want,' he said again.

'Thank you,' I said quietly. I wasn't quite sure how we were going to work things out. I assumed he'd give us time to pay so I could choose the dress I really wanted. I worked out that I could afford the pink-and-white lace dress if I paid it up in instalments and I hoped that was what he meant when he said he'd take care of it.

I couldn't help but pick out a matching bonnet and coat, and a little pair of tights too. It goes without saying that they were all things Nikitta would have loved. It was unthinkable that Kelsey-May could be laid to rest in anything she wouldn't have approved of.

I took the clothes to the till and the assistant began to cash them up. I could feel my heart rate quickening as I saw the total mount up on the screen and I wondered if I'd misunderstood the owner. Maybe he expected me to pay in full after all and he wouldn't give me the chance to pay it up over time. Embarrassed, I fumbled in my bag for my purse. Paul's mum was rooting around in her bag too. She could sense how uptight I was and she didn't want me to be any more distressed than I was already. 'I'll take care of it, Marce,' she whispered, fishing out her purse. 'Leave it to me, please.'

When I looked up, the owner was already behind the counter. 'Please,' he said. 'Put your purse away.' Tenderly, he picked up the clothes, one by one, and placed them into a pink bag. He passed it along the counter to me with a weak half-smile.

'I'm sorry,' I said. 'I don't understand. When would you like me to pay for these?'

'I don't want you to pay for them, madam,' he replied. 'These are from us, to you and your family.' He paused, before adding, 'With our deepest sympathies.'

Chapter Nine
The Scene of the Crime

I cried for a long time after the man in the boutique gave me the clothes for free. It's a strange world we live in where the most horrendous acts of evil can inspire the most amazing kindness. I was virtually a stranger to this man. I didn't even know his name, though, of course, by now he would have learned mine. Yet I don't think he'll ever know how much such a simple gesture meant to us. Nothing could dull the pain of our loss but it gave me the smallest crumb of comfort to think that Kelsey-May would make her final journey in such a pretty outfit.

He wasn't the only person who moved us to tears with thoughtfulness. There were two little rogues on Broadmead Park who couldn't have been more than ten years old but they were always out on the streets, causing trouble. When Paul opened the door to them a few nights later, his first feeling was mild irritation. He assumed they somehow hadn't heard about Nikitta, or they'd come to the wrong door and they wanted to play some kind of prank on us.

His heart almost melted when the smaller of the two produced a bunch of flowers and gave them to him. The other sheepishly handed over a bucket filled with coins.

'We've been collecting for you,' he said.

'We went round all of the houses,' his friend added proudly. 'We hope you like the flowers.'

Paul was speechless.

'We remember Nikitta and Missy,' the first boy went on. 'Missy was cute. We'll miss them.'

'Thank you so much, boys,' he said. When he came back into the house and told me what had happened, I couldn't speak. I think that, if I'd tried to get any more words out, I would have broken down again. We still had so many flowers but I made a special place in the living room for those ones.

At this point, Luke was out collecting money too. He'd made it his mission to raise enough for a bench for Nikitta, Kelsey-May and Missy. It was a focus for him and an excuse to get out and about for some fresh air when the atmosphere in the house became too stifling. In the end, he raised around £700. Paul and I were so proud of him.

It was around this time when Ian Hodgkinson explained that Whant would soon be appearing at Caerphilly Magistrates Court for a preliminary hearing. The charges against him – murder, rape, child destruction and arson – would be read out to him. Then a date would be set for him to enter a plea. If he admitted his crimes, he would be sentenced accordingly. If he didn't, preparations would be made for a trial. Ian warned us that, if the case did go to trial, it could last a month, if not longer, but we were still living day to day. We hadn't even laid our three precious girls to rest. I couldn't yet comprehend the idea of sitting in a court-room, listening to every detail of how they'd died.

Paul and Ryan decided they would make the short journey to Caerphilly with the FLOs. It was a pretty traumatic experience and when Paul told me about it later, I was glad I had stayed at home. Lots of our friends and family turned up to support us, which was lovely, but emotions were running very high and when the prison van carrying Whant drove into the car park, some of them started banging on the side and shouting abuse at him. This really stressed Paul out, as he didn't want anyone to take the law into their own hands, as it might give Whant's defence team some ammunition. He had to try to calm everyone down before they went into the court.

Things got even worse when everybody went inside. Whant's parents had turned up and the court staff put everyone into the same holding room, mistakenly thinking they were friends of ours. Whant's dad gave Paul the filthiest of looks – Paul says he almost felt like he was the criminal. He had a word with a helpful usher and they were moved but it really set everyone on edge for the rest of the day.

In the end, Whant was only in court for a few minutes. He spoke only to confirm his name and to say he had no fixed address, which was strange, as we were sure he was living with his girlfriend. Apparently, he shook his head as the charges were being read out and then he was led back to the van in handcuffs. It would be several months before he'd appear in court again.

I think it was around this time that I started to become plagued by doubts. I didn't like Whant – I never had – but I became tortured with all sorts of alternative scenarios. What if the police had made a huge mistake and arrested the wrong man? What if the monster who took our girls was still roaming the streets, free to harm other innocent young women?

We still weren't allowed to know much about the forensic evidence, so we didn't realise how compelling it was. Sometimes I'd make lists of names of people who I thought could have had a grudge against Nikitta or Ryan. My imagination was running wild and most of the people I thought of popped into my head for ridiculous reasons – friends Nikitta had fallen out with years ago over typical teenage stuff.

'Marcia,' Ian would say gently. 'I think we've got our man.'

As Whant had been charged, the press were now restricted in what they could say about the case – again, to make sure he got a fair trial. But they were still camped outside of Nikitta's flat because they wanted a photo of us going to see the tributes people had left there. I really wanted to see them but I didn't want to face the press. Like I said before, I'm a private person and the idea of showing my emotions to the whole country filled me with horror.

'This might sound strange,' Ian said, 'but if the press can

get just one picture of you all at the flat, they'll probably leave you alone. There's not much they can really say now until Whant is in court next.'

'So if they can get one picture of us, they'll go away?' I asked.

'They'll still be around,' Ian said. 'They'll probably knock on your door and try to get some stories from you that they can use after the case has finished. But things won't be so intense.'

I nodded. 'OK,' I replied. 'We'll go and have a quick look.'

Even though Nikitta's flat was just a short walk from our house, Ian took us round in the car. It meant we could quickly escape if we felt overwhelmed by all of the cameras. Luke decided he wanted to come with us, so I promised myself I would try to be strong, as hard as it might be.

It was the first time we'd dared to venture to Nikitta's street since the day of the fire, despite the fact it was so close. As we drew up to the flat, my stomach lurched violently. Out of the car windows I could see how the building's white exterior had been blackened by the smoke. The violence of the flames had caused the bedroom windows to smash – something I'd been too preoccupied to notice on the day. The remaining windows were covered by thick wooden boards. A solitary police officer, wearing a high-visibility vest, stood guard at the door. When the car drew up, he bowed his head solemnly.

I was brought back to earth with a jolt as Ian opened the car door to let me out.

'Ready?' he asked.

I nodded. In an almost dreamlike state, I wrapped my arm around Luke and clasped Paul's hand in mine. Suddenly I caught sight of the sea of bouquets and teddies. There must literally have been hundreds of them. I was vaguely aware of the cameras sounding, of the intense heat of the flashbulbs on my face, but I didn't feel intimidated or anxious as I'd feared I might do. The press just didn't seem important – they were the least of our problems.

I didn't know where to go first. There were so many cards and messages and I wanted to read them all. I picked up a bouquet of gorgeous yellow roses at random – Nikitta's favourite – and read the card attached to it.

'You were like the Paris Hilton of Broadmead Park,' it read. 'You were so glam. We will really miss you and Missy.'

I had to swallow hard to keep the sobs at bay but I managed not to cry as I carefully placed the flowers back on top of the pile. As I reached down, my eyes were drawn to a lovely pink teddy. It was a little weather-beaten and the rainfall meant it had become dirty and faded but it still looked so pretty to me. I thought of our beautiful little Kelsey-May and imagined her all cwtched up with it in her cot. It had a card taped to its back and, as I opened it, I realised it was from the family of a little girl who had been in my class a few years back.

'Miss Grender,' she'd written, in careful, childish hand-writing. I did a quick calculation in my head and figured she must have been about nine or ten by now. 'I was in your class and I remember you. I am sorry about Nikitta and Kelsey-May xxx.'

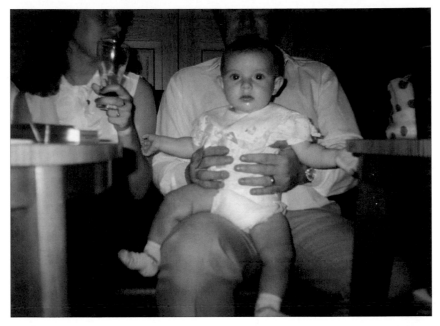

Above: Baby Nikitta on her father's knee at the Dean Street Social Club.

Below left: At Paul's parents' house aged three.

Below right: 'Mother Christmas' giving a present to Nikitta at a Christmas party.

Above: An early driving lesson with cousin Gareth.

Below left: Aged seven, proudly holding a certificate at Ringland Primary School.

Below right: Nikitta on Christmas Day 2009 with her baby cousin Anna-Keigh.

Above: Nikitta was a bridesmaid at Paul's brother Michael's wedding to Melanie, who is holding Nikitta's cousin, Iestyn.

Below: With Paul's father.

Above left: With Luke at Paul's brother Matthew's wedding, where Nikitta was also a bridesmaid.

Above right: With her fiancé, Ryan.

Below: A family photo of Nikitta with Luke and Paul's parents, June and Jim.

The words were so simple but so moving. I just couldn't believe a little girl of her age had taken the time to come down and pay her respects. It made me angry too, though. Why did this sweet little girl have to grow up in a world where such evil existed? She should never have had to leave a card for my murdered daughter and granddaughter because it should never have happened.

By now Paul's arms were around my waist and he was sobbing into my neck. Luke was crying too and I drew him to me. Suddenly, I snapped out of the trance I was in. I became aware of all of the faces around us and all the cameras pointing towards us; I felt like I was in some kind of sick pantomime.

That's when the anxiety came, thick and fast. My breathing quickened and my heart began to hammer, as if it might burst out of my chest. I'm not sure if I was about to cry or not, but I didn't want to hang around to find out. I craned my neck to look for Ian and within seconds, he was by my side.

'We need to go,' I said. 'We need to go. This is enough. Now we need to go.'

Without hesitation, he bundled us back into the car and I slumped down on the seat, resting my head in my hands. As we drove away I didn't look out of the window at the flat.

I'm not sure if it was a few days or a few weeks before Ian offered us the chance to go into the flat itself. Presumably, the police had retrieved everything they needed for the investigation. He asked if we'd like to go and gather what we could salvage of Nikitta's belongings.

'Yes,' I said without hesitation. I knew how hard it would

be to go back in there, to see the destruction wreaked by Whant in the home my daughter had so lovingly built for her little family and to stand in the room where she'd taken her last breath, imagining her terror and the sound of her screams. But I had to do it – not just for Nikitta, but also for Kelsey-May. All of her things – the things we had so excitedly bought for her – were in there. I just couldn't bear the thought of them festering in a dirty, smoke-damaged room before being chucked on a rubbish skip. Kelsey-May deserved better than that.

Ryan wanted to come too and we couldn't say no really, as lots of his things were still in there. Ian was with us and a man from the council let us in. He was really lovely. As he turned the key in the door, he told us we could call him any time of the day or night and he'd come in and open up for us.

The first thing that hit us was the smell of smoke. It had been a few weeks since the fire but it was so strong that I almost gagged. Although there were far fewer people there than there had been the day we'd gone to see the tributes, I still didn't want to break down in front of anyone other than Paul. I clasped his hand tightly, my palms sweaty.

The boards on the windows had made it so dark that the man from the council had to turn on a flashlight to light our way to the bedroom. I'm not sure how I felt as he opened the door and let us pass through. It was like I was in some sort of parallel universe; I was going through the motions but I wasn't really there, I had stopped living and merely existed.

There was a little more light in Nikitta's room than there

was in any of the other rooms, as the windows had been smashed by the fire.

For a few seconds, I just stood in the doorway, rooted to the spot.

Everything from the bed frame to the curtains was completely black. We'd be able to salvage very little, if anything. But that, momentarily, faded to the back of my mind.

This was it. This was where Nikitta had breathed for the last time, lying on this bed, in this room. Would we ever know what really happened in those awful last minutes? It would have been dark – so dark – and if he'd broken in, she'd have been confused and scared to find him towering over her. Or had she let him in, thinking he was Ryan, only for him to do the unthinkable?

Ryan was standing in the corner of the room, looking pallid. Suddenly, I remembered his lost keys. Maybe Whant had planned his attack for weeks, keeping the keys safely tucked in his pocket and waiting for the right moment to pounce. A wave of rage swept over me. Why hadn't Ryan been at home protecting Nikitta? I knew he was just a lad and that he could have never predicted that Whant would do this but I still couldn't forgive him for leaving her home alone that night.

She'd have tried to fight him off – of that I was certain – but she wouldn't have stood a chance. Whant was a bulky brute, whom I'd heard took steroids, and she was a small, fragile, heavily pregnant teenager. There would have been no contest as he overwhelmed her on the bed, drunk with lust and God knows what else. I tried not to flinch as I imagined him pawing at her, his horrible eyes wide with sick satisfaction.

For the first time, I understood what Paul had meant when he said he knew why Whant had killed her. If he'd raped our daughter, she'd never have let it lie. She would have been traumatised, of course, but there was no bloody way she'd have swept it under the carpet and pretended it hadn't happened. She would have come running to her dad and he would have killed Whant with his bare hands if he'd had to.

It was only as I surveyed the devastation of the bedroom that I realised what a coward Whant really was. He was willing to attack a vulnerable, pregnant woman in the dead of night, while armed with a knife, but he wasn't willing to face the consequences: he wasn't brave enough.

I can't begin to imagine what must have been going through Paul's mind. Nikitta was the apple of his eye and the idea of anyone laying a finger on her would have been ripping him to shreds. But in that moment, all I was aware of was my own pain, as I dug my nails deep into his hand.

I don't think I was crying. I can't say for certain but I can't remember feeling the tears rolling down my cheeks. My grief on that day wasn't the same raw, hysterical agony I'd experienced when the police called round to tell us Nikitta had been in the house, or when I'd collapsed by her side in the police mortuary. It was more like something was gnawing at me, deep in the pit of my stomach, slowly but surely eating me alive.

From that day onwards, I knew that feeling would be

with me until the day I died, burrowing away quietly in the background as a constant reminder that things would never be OK again, no matter what happened.

I wanted Whant locked away – of course I did – but however long a prison sentence he got, we'd have the real life sentence.

We didn't have the energy to begin clearing out the bedroom that day, so we quickly had a look around the other rooms. We didn't go into Kelsey-May's nursery in the end. That would have been too painful, so it was a job for another day.

When we entered the kitchen, the tears sprang to my eyes. The man from the council had to turn the flashlights back on so we could see, as the windows in there were boarded up too.

Nikitta had been pretty tidy but there were a few dishes on the draining board and a joint of meat had been left to defrost on the side. It was just as she'd left it. I imagined what would have been going through her mind as she drifted into sleep that night – what she'd planned to cook with the meat, which had greyed with the passing weeks.

In the living room there was some washing that had been drying on the radiators – nothing much, all charred black now, of course.

'Can we come back another day?' I asked Ian. 'I want to get Kelsey-May's things. I want to make sure I can save all I can.'

'Of course,' he told me. 'You heard what the guy said – you can come whenever you want. Have you had enough for today?'

I nodded wordlessly. As we walked out of the flat, the daylight and fresh air hit me and I felt almost dizzy. I could still smell the smoke on my clothes and in my hair.

When we got home a few minutes later, I dropped Paul's hand and sprinted upstairs, closing the bathroom door behind mc. I reached to turn the shower on and peeled off my winter clothes, tossing them carelessly on the floor.

As the warm water hit my face, I felt no relief. All I could smell was smoke – thick, heavy, black smoke. I reached for the soap and began to scrub myself hard, trying to rid every pore of the stench. Nausea overwhelmed me and I retched but I wasn't sick.

I tipped my hair into the water and squeezed out a huge dollop of shampoo and rubbed it violently into my scalp, scratching my head so hard that it hurt. The steam was rising and the bathroom mirror clouded up as I rinsed my hair, still scrubbing and scrubbing my body until my arms and legs were red raw.

There were footsteps on the stairs, then a rap at the door.

'You OK, Marce?' Paul shouted.

'Mmm,' I managed to reply, though, of course, I wasn't OK. I'd never be OK ever again. I felt breathless and panicky, so I opened my mouth, desperate to get some air into my lungs. My mouth filled with water and, for a second, I felt like I was drowning.

I wondered what it would feel like to drown; to lie on top of the ocean and let my lungs fill with seawater as I disappeared beneath the surface, sinking without trace. At that moment, it seemed a peaceful and calming scenario; a release from the pain that was consuming me: the torment that wouldn't let up until my dying day.

Of course, it wasn't an option. I couldn't sink beneath the surface. I had to stay there, fighting to keep my head above water, every day struggling for air. Paul needed me, Luke needed me, my parents needed me – and Nikitta needed me to keep going for them.

As I turned the dial on the shower the water stopped with a sharp jolt. I stepped onto the bathmat and pulled my towel around me, my hair sticking to my cheeks. For a second I stood in the middle of the bathroom, not quite sure what to do.

The bile was rising in my throat once more and I thought again that I might be sick. I contemplated reaching for the toilet bowl but my stomach settled after a few seconds. Instead, I climbed back into the shower and turned the water back on.

I could still smell smoke.

Chapter Ten

Our Last Goodbye

I had another four showers that day. Each time, I scrubbed and scrubbed my skin until it was red raw but the stench of the flat still seemed to seep out of my pores.

The next evening, Paul and I decided to go to Asda for some groceries. It was a simple task, but to me it felt like climbing Everest. It seemed so wrong; so sinful. How could we walk around the supermarket like a normal family when Nikitta wasn't here? But we had to eat and we couldn't shut ourselves away forever, so we didn't have a choice.

At first I felt like I was coping as we piled bread and milk and other essentials into our trolley. I wasn't even thinking about what I was buying, I was just going through the motions.

'Why don't you get yourself some new boots?' Paul said. I think he was trying to cheer me up but I just felt flat.

'Remember Nikitta borrowed yours and didn't give them back? The little bugger!'

We both laughed weakly. She had loved to steal my shoes and clothes.

But as we turned the corner into the clothes section, I knew we'd made a huge mistake. There in front of us was a sale rail with some discounted clothes. Most of them were for kids and there were a few baby dresses, pink and frilly like the ones I couldn't stop buying for Kelsey-May.

I abandoned my trolley, right there and then, and ran right out into the car park. I'm not sure what happened next. I can only assume Paul hurriedly paid for the shopping and drove me home. The next thing I remember is being locked in the bathroom, slumped on the floor, crying until my face hurt.

I wasn't quite sure what to do with myself or all of the emotions I was feeling, so I went into my room and grabbed a beautiful blue notebook I had bought for Nikitta one Christmas. I almost smiled as I remembered how she'd torn a page from it and written us a note to tell us she was leaving home on one of the many times she'd escaped to live with Ryan. My heart ached. I'd been so mad at her for running away. It seemed so silly now. If only I could have her back, I didn't feel like I'd ever be mad at her for anything again.

My thoughts came tumbling out onto the page. If I couldn't talk to Nikitta – if I couldn't hold her in my arms – I could write to her. It gave me a shred of comfort to know that Nikitta had touched the pages.

You should be a mum, now, Nikitta. Ryan should be a dad, Luke an uncle, Dad a Grancha and me a Nanna. I should have been there with you in hospital, while you were bringing your daughter, our granddaughter, into the world – our baby, Kelsey-May. She is beautiful. Our two girls. I want to hold and kiss you and be Nanna. We're all thinking the same thing, all thinking of you, Kelsey-May and Missy. Why you?

In the privacy of my own room, I cried the tears I couldn't bear to cry in public. My face was hot and sticky and my hair stuck to my cheeks as sweat dripped down onto my neck. But I kept writing.

Hope you are all safe, my angels. I realise you are probably not at peace, but that will come in time, I promise you, sweethearts, especially when you are all together and justice has been served. I can assure you, Nikitta, he will pay for what he has done, sweetheart.

A few days later, we were told the bodies of our girls could be released to us and we could begin to plan a funeral. Some people say that a funeral gives you closure; that it helps you grieve. I couldn't understand how I could ever get closure and I didn't want to grieve because I still couldn't comprehend how this had happened. I didn't want it to be real and a funeral would only hammer the horrible truth home.

But, once again, I had to put my feelings to one side and find the steely facade I'd come to know so well over recent months. Our girls deserved the best send-off we could give them and I had to make sure the day was as close to perfect as possible. Wondering what Nikitta would be thinking, I picked up my diary. I wrote,

Hi, my three angels. Thinking of you all always. We had the call today – the call we've all been waiting for. We can finally put you all to rest. I know it's taken ages, Keet, but they need every piece of evidence they can get. It's almost over, darling. You will be together soon, sweetheart. It's been hard knowing you are separated and it's NOT fair. I'm hoping you will be at peace soon, baby girl.

I always wonder exactly what you'll be thinking at certain times, Keet. I wonder what you'll be thinking now. Are you proud of how everyone is doing or are you angry or sad? I wish I knew, Keet!

It had been tearing me apart thinking that Nikitta, Kelsey-May and Missy were not side by side. We decided that we wanted to have Nikitta and Kelsey-May cremated but that we'd buy a plot at the local cemetery where we could bury their ashes. It was so important to us that we had somewhere we could visit them and speak to them. There was absolutely no question that Missy would be laid to rest with them. She was part of our family and she'd been so loyal to Nikitta in life. Even in death, we could never have separated them.

'We'll have to choose a coffin,' Paul said softly. I held my head in my hands. Just a few weeks ago, I had been choosing baby clothes. Now I would have to pick out a casket for my daughter and granddaughter and our beloved little dog. I wanted to run upstairs, shut my bedroom door and hide under the covers forever but I had to do this for Nikitta.

At first I thought of buying her a pink coffin. She had been so girly and it had been her favourite colour, but when we went to the funeral directors, all of the pink caskets looked cheap and tatty.

'No,' I told Paul, shaking my head. 'She'd have hated them. And that makes me hate them.'

Paul agreed. In the end, we chose white instead. It looked much classier.

'Let's have the coffin carried by a coach and horses,' I said to Paul. 'Wouldn't that be lovely?'

His face fell as he slipped an arm around my waist. 'Yes,' he replied, catching the lump in his throat. 'But Marce, we can't afford it.'

I pulled away from him, tears stinging my eyes. How could he think of money at a time like this? Couldn't we just give our girls the best send-off we could and then worry about it later?

It was as if he'd read my mind. I suppose when you've known someone so well for so long, you can almost tap into their thoughts.

'I've worked out a plan with the funeral director,' he explained, 'where we can pay it up, bit by bit. But it's already costing thousands, Marce. And we already owe money left, right and centre.'

I hated to admit he had a point. We'd only been off work

for a few weeks and already we were running into debt. We could barely afford to heat the house and put food on the table. We were keeping our heads above water because of the generosity of family and friends, who were all rallying round to help. There was no chance either of us would be able to go back to work anytime soon – we could barely find the energy to get dressed. Our financial situation was only going to get worse.

'I'm sorry,' Paul said, pulling me close to him again. He had tears in his eyes too. 'I wish we could. But you know we have to draw a line somewhere.'

'I know,' I replied eventually. 'It's just so bloody hard.'

Even though we're not religious people, we decided on a church service. We picked St John's Church in the Maindee area of Newport, near to where my Nan and Grancha had lived when I was a little girl. We'd been told to expect hundreds of mourners and it seemed like the only place big enough to accommodate them all. The local vicar, a nice woman called Helen, came round to chat to us about Nikitta.

'Well, she was very vain!' I said. 'But she had every bloody right to be. She was gorgeous, everyone says so.'

We decided the service would be on Tuesday, 9 March, followed by a private burial a few days later. In the days leading up to the funeral, things seemed blacker than they ever had before. There was a steady stream of people coming in and out of the house but I'd never felt so alone. Even when Paul wrapped his arms around me in bed at night, I thought of Nikitta. I wasn't sure if there was an afterlife but I wondered if she could somehow see us and sense how we were feeling. It sounds strange but I worried about her. I worried that, wherever she was, she was lonely. Of course, she had Kelsey-May and Missy but surely she'd be missing us, and Luke, and Ryan?

The next evening, I overheard an innocent conversation between two people in the house – I can't remember who now. One was telling the other about how she'd gone to the hospital with her daughter when she'd given birth. I'm sure they didn't realise I was within earshot, as the living room was packed, as usual, but it was like my ears were instinctively drawn to their conversation.

I didn't want to cry in front of everyone so I clenched my stomach muscles along with the cheeks of my arse, gritted my teeth and gripped my coffee cup so tightly I lost the feeling in my right hand. By the time the house finally emptied and I went upstairs to bed, my body ached with the tension. I got out my pen and Nikitta's notebook but all I could see was Whant and his unbearable, smug, disgusting face. For a moment – just for a moment – I allowed myself to imagine it wasn't real. My mind flashed back to the night on the sofa, when I'd made Nikitta take my hand while we watched TV and I'd sung her the song she'd loved as a child. I could still feel her hand in mine and picture her lovely face. I could hear her mocking me for being soppy but I still hoped that she was secretly enjoying it too. My tears dripped onto the notepaper, smudging the ink as I tried to write. There was only one thought inside my head now:

*BASTARD, BASTARD, BASTARD, BASTARD,
BASTARD, BASTARD.*

The day of the funeral was cold and grey. I didn't sleep much the night before. As I showered and climbed into my clothes – black trousers and a black jacket, with a yellow rose pinned to the lapel – I felt like a zombie. The heady mixture of grief and sleep deprivation was something I had come to know all too well and it now felt almost normal.

I could hear people starting to come into the house as I brushed my hair, salty tears running down my cheeks. I had to get ready to face the world. As the days and weeks went on, the intensity of my loss never weakened. It only got stronger, as every moment that passed was another moment without Nikitta. However, my desire to keep my feelings to myself did start to grow. It felt wrong to show the world how much I missed her, as if I was somehow betraying her. So I dried my eyes and made my way downstairs, ready to face the day no mother should ever have to face.

There must have been at least thirty people there already and nearly everyone was wearing pink. The men had pink shirts or ties, while the women were wearing pink blouses, jackets and scarves. Ian had warned us that the press would be out in force at the funeral and that it would be good to have something to distinguish our family and close friends, so we could be kept in separate parts of the church. We'd decided pink clothes and yellow roses would be best, as Nikitta had loved both.

Uncle Paul had brought round some spare cups and

an extra kettle so he and Auntie Tracey could make teas and coffees for everyone but the morning passed in a blur as the house got busier and busier and soon people were standing in the garden too. Before we knew it, the funeral cars were outside. An old friend of Paul's, who ran a local limousine company, kindly let us use them for free. Paul had planned everything with military precision, from who was travelling in which car to the route we'd take to the church. I'm not sure how he managed it but he later told me he was on autopilot.

When I first caught sight of the white coffin through the window of the black hearse, I felt like someone was slowly ripping my insides out, killing me, bit by bit.

I don't think I said a single word on the way there. Luke was sitting next to me and I had my arm around him. There were so many cars parked outside our house that it took us ages to get out of Broadmead Park.

When we pulled up outside the church, I saw the police officers standing guard but I was so detached from reality that I didn't even realise they were there for the funeral. I just thought it was a coincidence.

As we climbed out of the car, I suddenly became aware of the huge crowds that had amassed. The churchyard was a sea of pink and the crowd parted as we approached. There were a few soft sobs.

Paul, Ryan and the other pallbearers carried the white coffin into the church and I followed behind with Luke. I had to take my eyes off the other mourners and fix them on the church doorway. I bit my cheek hard so I wouldn't cry.

I could taste the blood in my mouth as I held Luke to me as we walked up the stairs behind the coffin.

The church was full to bursting point but I tried not to look at anyone, apart from Paul. As he helped lay the coffin on its stand, I could see the strain on his face. I thought of the day of the fire and how he'd tried to get past the firefighters to get to Nikitta. He would have laid down his own life if it could have brought our daughter back. I would have done the same, in a heartbeat.

Why couldn't it have been me in that coffin? Why Nikitta? Why Kelsey-May? I didn't go to church often, but now that I was there, I cursed God for taking them and leaving me behind.

Luke had grabbed hold of my arm and he was sobbing into my jacket. My cheeks burned with shame at the thoughts I'd been thinking as I stroked his head. I had to keep going for him; he was my reason for going on. I caught my breath as we shuffled into our seats.

We'd asked for a photo of Nikitta to be placed at the front of the church. I couldn't take my eyes off it. Her brown eyes shone and her smile lit up the room. It felt like she was right there, looking at us. I wanted to jump up and grab her, hug her to me and never let go. But, of course, I couldn't: it was just a photograph and she was just a memory.

A few days before the funeral, we'd been approached by the Newport Male Voice Choir. They'd asked if they could sing for Nikitta and we'd been so touched by the request. The service began with their rendition of 'Amazing Grace'. It was so beautiful that it made the hairs on the back of my neck stand up.

'We are here to say a formal goodbye to a happy, lively young woman and her much-loved and much-wanted baby,' Helen, the vicar, said after the music had stopped. 'If the world was as it should be, and as our loving God desires it to be, there would be no need for a funeral today. Both Nikitta and Kelsey-May had everything to live for. There was so much that they could have done and been and given.'

I swallowed hard.

'Their time on Earth should not have been so cruelly cut short,' she went on. 'We are here in the shadow of a terrible injustice and act of evil and we cannot pretend otherwise.'

There had been so many people who had wanted to stand up and pay tribute to Nikitta and we were overwhelmed. It's not an easy thing to speak in public, not least on such an emotional day. But in the end, we decided we couldn't have everyone, or the service would have lasted all day. We asked Big Luke and Patrick and Cheryl's daughter, Shirelle, to speak. They'd both been very close to Nikitta and we were sure they'd give her fitting tributes.

Shirelle spoke of all the Saturday evenings she and Nikitta had spent together when they were children, making up little plays to perform to the adults downstairs, and how they'd both been so excited to be bridesmaids at her parents' wedding.

When Big Luke began to speak, I could hear people sniffling around me. He told the congregation how Nikitta had been like a sister to him and that, when he'd realised he was gay as a teenager, she was the first person he'd told.

They'd fought like brother and sister but only because they were so close.

Then it was our turn. Paul and I could never have spoken publicly; it was hard enough keeping upright. But we had so much to say about Nikitta and it wouldn't have felt right not to say it. We were so grateful when Paul's brother Mike volunteered to read our words for us. As he walked up to the pulpit, my heart started to race. He looked so composed but I knew that, as with me, it was all a front: he had to be calm because he knew how much this meant to Paul and me. I suspect he cried many private tears, but to us, he was a rock. Over the next few months we'd soon discover just how big a support he'd be.

He took a deep breath as he opened the piece of paper on which I'd carefully written the words a few nights previously.

'Nikitta will be laughing at all this attention,' he said finally. 'She loved the limelight and who can blame her? She was a beautiful young woman. We're missing you, Keet,' His voice wavered but only for a split second, 'even though you were a pain in the rear. You made us constantly laugh and cry.

'You would have been a fantastic mum. Kelsey-May, our first granddaughter, we didn't have the chance to spend time with you, sweetheart. Missy, we're missing your muddy footprints – barking, toys and hairs everywhere. We're missing you all so much.'

I could hear some sobs ringing out around me, from our family and some friends in the rows behind. I fixed my eyes on Nikitta's beautiful picture, willing her to give me – and Mike – the strength to keep going.

'They say love hurts and you'll miss it when it's gone,' he continued, reading my words slowly but clearly. I thought of how my tears had dripped onto the page as I'd written them. They had sprung to my eyes again but I was just about holding it together. 'We never thought that could be true. It's killing us that you're gone, sweetheart.'

Luke was sobbing softly now and Paul had his head in his hands.

'There will never, ever be a day when we don't think about you – we'll never stop thinking of you,' Mike went on. 'We miss you and we love you, Nikitta. Rest in peace, sweetheart, and look after our granddaughter, Kelsey-May, and Missy. Good night, God bless and sweet dreams, sweetheart. Love you.'

The choir then sang 'O Great Redeemer' before it was time for Nikitta's coffin to be carried from the church. I'd asked for the Adele version of 'Make You Feel My Love' to be played as we walked out behind it. It's such a beautiful song but I've never been able to listen to it since that day.

The sobs were much louder as we walked down the aisle and out of the church. On the way out, I caught the eye of one of the members of the choir. He was a grown man who didn't know us at all but he had tears in his eyes.

'Thank you very much,' I mouthed and he bowed his head respectfully.

The cold air hit me as we got outside. I was still holding Luke close as we walked with the procession behind the coffin. I could hear the clicking of the cameras and feel the heat of the flashbulbs. I knew they were zooming in on me and that I'd be in all the papers the next day but I couldn't have cared less. Nikitta and I had been so similar in some ways and so different in others. While she'd loved being the centre of attention, I couldn't imagine anything worse. Before all this happened, the idea of my face being plastered all over the tabloids – not to mention the Internet – would have filled me with absolute horror. I was so private that I didn't even have a Facebook page. Now I'd have had my photo taken for every newspaper in the country if it would have brought the girls back.

As soon as the coffin had been lowered into the hearse, I made a beeline for the funeral car. Paul was being grabbed by people, who were hugging him and crying. They meant well, of course, but I had begun to feel claustrophobic and I couldn't stand to be around so many hysterical people. I was like a ticking time bomb of emotion, ready to go off at any moment. Luke stayed outside with his dad, while I sat in the car on my own for twenty-five minutes.

Away from all the commotion I felt much safer. I could hear people asking where I was but I didn't have the energy to get back out, so I figured they could find me themselves. It was hardly like I'd gone far.

While there were hundreds of people at the church, it was mainly family and close friends who came with us to the crematorium in Cwmbran. Ryan had chosen a song he and Nikitta had liked from a film they'd watched to be played as the white coffin disappeared behind the curtain. I can't even remember what it was called now. I don't think I even remember it playing as I watched the surreal scene unfold before my eyes.

Paul had been so strong because he knew I was dying inside but this was a bit too much for him and he broke down. In a trance I just stood there, vacantly, waiting to wake up. I was convinced someone would tap me on the shoulder and say, 'Don't worry, Marce. It's over now, you dreamt it all. What a horrible nightmare, eh?'

Nikitta's ashes would be buried at the plot we'd chosen a few days later, so we invited everyone back to one of the local pubs for a few drinks. It was the done thing but the last thing I wanted to do was socialise. I've never been much of a drinker and I don't like the lack of control that comes with having one too many. There were a lot of emotional people and they were only going to get more emotional as the alcohol started to flow.

Somehow, I got through the afternoon but I hated every minute of it. It seemed so odd to be sitting in a bar surrounded by all of our family and friends when Nikitta wasn't there. It's odd how you can feel so lonely in such a big crowd. After a few hours, I was glad to get home and shut myself in my room, where I wrote to Nikitta.

It was your day, Keet. What a turnout! I couldn't believe it. I wouldn't look at anyone because I knew I wouldn't be able to handle it. My focus was you, your dad, and Luke. I couldn't take my eyes off your photo, sweetheart. Your dad has finally had a good cry today.

I'm glad he's getting some of it out of his system. What did you think of the Welsh choir, Keet? I thought they were amazing.

Love you loads, sweetheart. Love you, Kelsey-May. We've got over one hurdle – just one more to go with the burial on Monday and then the long-awaited trial of that fucking twat and we can get justice for you all. And we WILL get justice for you, sweetheart, okay? Unfortunately, it won't bring you back, baby girls, but it's justice in the eyes of the law. If only it could bring you back, if only. Love you, Keeta, and always will xxx.

The burial was a quiet affair. Our parents came along and some close family and friends. Helen, our local vicar, said a few words and we released some pink balloons as the ashes were lowered into the ground. It gave me the smallest crumb of comfort to know that Nikitta, Kelsey-May and Missy were now together.

As the pink balloons sailed high above Newport, I noticed a white feather floating in the air. I was desperate to believe in something – anything – that meant I'd one day be reunited with my girls and that day, I clung to the hope that it was Nikitta's way of telling me everything was alright; that our three precious angels were at peace.

Chapter Eleven

Movements of a Monster

As we were burying our girls, the police were working furiously behind the scenes to prove beyond reasonable doubt that Whant had been responsible for their deaths. On the face of it, it seemed like an open-and-shut case. His DNA had been found on Nikitta's body and traces of her blood could be detected in his car and on her clothes but it wasn't as simple as that.

Whant would try everything he could to get off – it was like some kind of sick game to him. DCS Ronayne and his team had to make sure they had left no stone unturned and that they had an answer for everything his defence team might throw at them, should the case go to trial.

All Paul and I really knew was that the police had recovered forensic evidence linking Whant to the scene of Nikitta's murder. Still, they sounded pretty convinced they'd got their man. We had no idea how hard they were working to explore every possible aspect of the case.

At first, when Whant had been interviewed, he'd denied having sex with Nikitta. He didn't know then about the vaginal swabs but maybe he'd guessed the police were onto him because he said something really strange.

'I haven't had sex with Nikitta Grender,' he said flatly. 'But every time I have sex, I think about having sex with her.'

When I found out he'd said this – months later, just before the court case – I was absolutely disgusted. Of course, it was obvious he found Nikitta attractive because he'd leered over the private pictures of her on her phone. She was beautiful – every man round our way fancied her. Still, the thought of the cogs turning in his head as it filled with sick fantasies made me retch.

He went on to tell the interviewer that he and Nikitta had once met up at a bus stop.

'We had a kiss and a cuddle,' he added. 'Nothing more.'

It was a complete lie, naturally. Nikitta couldn't stand to look at him, never mind hug and kiss him. It would never have happened in a thousand years but she was a pawn in his sick game. Whant was creating a history between them that never existed, to make it plausible that they could have had consensual sex. He was covering his tracks in case the police found the evidence he'd so desperately tried to hide.

When told the police had forensic evidence that he'd slept with Nikitta, he said nothing, though. He simply complained of feeling unwell and refused to answer any more questions. Again, he had taken the coward's way out and it would be months before he came up with an explanation of any sort.

DCS Ronayne and his team knew he'd try to say the sex was consensual if he decided to plead not guilty and let the case go to trial. Experts are divided on how long traces of semen can survive in the vagina – some say five days, while others claim seven. From a forensic point of view, Whant could have technically had sex with Nikitta at any time in the week leading up to her death and it was highly likely that he'd try to argue that she had agreed to sleep with him a few nights previously. The case was highly confidential so we didn't know what the officers were trying to establish. Had we been aware of this, we would have found it absolutely incredulous. Whant made Nikitta's skin crawl – never in a million years would she have willingly had sex with him. But potential jurors wouldn't know Nikitta or how much she disliked him, so the police had to show that the only opportunity Whant would have had to have sex with our daughter was on the night she died.

It was a huge job and it took months. DCS Ronayne instructed officers to establish, if they could, that it wouldn't have been possible for this to have happened because they simply weren't together for long enough at any given time. Nikitta avoided Whant wherever possible but he did spend a lot of time at the flat and it would be very difficult to account for both of their movements for every minute of every day.

Officers trawled shopping bills and phone records, and spoke to friends, family and neighbours to piece things together. They did a sterling job – in the end, there was only a fifteen-minute window in which Whant was unaccounted for. Incredibly, an officer managed to obtain a statement from a known drug dealer saying that Whant had spent this time buying cocaine from him.

They'd managed to prove that Whant and Nikitta had only been in the same place for around ten or fifteen minutes in the week leading up to the fire. On the Friday evening he'd called at the flat with Ryan just before Nikitta had come round to our house with Missy and Jenna had picked her up (Ryan had wanted to get changed before they headed out to watch the rugby). Ryan told the police that Whant had a cigarette in the kitchen and barely spoke to Nikitta. Whant would challenge this version of events but that would come much later.

So what had really happened when he'd said he had gone out to get cigarettes from his grandmother?

After the rugby finished, Whant and Ryan had continued drinking. They'd gone to another pub, where they'd met the girls who had invited them back to the house party on Corelli Street. Whant had driven Ryan and the girls there. It hadn't bothered him in the slightest that he'd been drinking and taking cocaine when he got behind the wheel. He did so without a second thought for the passengers in his car or the other people on the road.

They arrived at the flat at about 2.20am. The police analysed Whant's phone records, which showed he'd been chatting to girls on Facebook all night. Bored of waiting for him to come home, his girlfriend had gone to bed.

It was some time around 4.30am that Whant decided he

was tired of the party. None of the girls seemed to be paying him any attention and that made him mad. The cocktail of alcohol and cocaine had turned him into a ticking time bomb of aggression and sexual desire. Presumably, he had thought one of the girls he'd picked up would be interested in him but they hardly gave him a second glance.

Ryan told the police that he and one of the girls had offered to go and pick up the cigarettes with Whant but he'd been adamant he wanted to go alone.

'Just stay here,' he'd said, stammering a little as he got the words out. 'I won't be long.'

Of course, it seemed obvious that he'd headed not for his grandmother's but for Nikitta's. CCTV footage appeared to back this up – a silver Ford Focus just like the one he'd drunkenly parked in Corelli Street was filmed driving in the direction of Broadmead Park just after 5am. A similar car was pictured driving back to Corelli Street around 6.15am. Whant had arrived back at the property at 6.30am, a short while after Ryan had phoned his girlfriend to see if he'd gone home.

But, as ever, it wasn't as simple as that. DCS Ronayne knew the defence would argue there were lots of silver Ford Focus cars in Newport. How could the police be sure it was Whant behind the wheel? And had he really gone to Nikitta's?

To establish this, they had to call on experts from the Transport Research Laboratory in Cardiff. Their experts could analyse the footage and decide if there were any features on Whant's car that would distinguish it from other similar vehicles.

Again, this was a painstaking process that took weeks to complete. DCS Ronayne and the Transport Research Laboratory agreed that an analyst with no knowledge of the case should watch the CCTV footage of the journey they believed Whant had taken. To establish if there were, indeed, any features that made his car stand out from other similar models, they would reconstruct the journey five times. They'd use the car in question and four dummy cars of the same colour, make and model as the one Whant had been driving on the night Nikitta died – almost identical but not quite.

This was far more complicated than it sounds. The cars had to be driven along the exact route Whant's car had taken but the lighting and weather conditions also had to be exactly as they were on the morning of Nikitta's death – or as close to exactly as possible. This took weeks to perfect, but eventually, police managed to pull the reconstruction off.

To the naked eye, the cars looked exactly the same but one of the lights on the rear number plate of Whant's car wasn't quite working. It was such a tiny detail and you'd have had to really strain your eyes to notice it, but the analyst spotted it almost immediately. In the reconstruction, the light was out at exactly the same place as it had been during the original journey.

There was a problem, though. There wasn't CCTV along the whole route so, although Whant was heading in the direction of Broadmead Park, there was no footage of him arriving in Nikitta's street, or of him leaving the house. DCS Ronayne worried the defence might seize upon this but the analysis did appear to prove one thing and that was that he hadn't gone to his grandmother's.

The fire alarm had begun to sound between 5.30am and 6am, so it was conceivable that Whant had gone to the flat, done the unthinkable and then returned to Corelli Street to continue partying, as if nothing had happened.

DCS Ronayne thought the defence might argue that Whant didn't have time to start the fire; that it had been an accident after all. This was tough, as experts were divided over how long it would have taken the smoke alarm to go off and wake Nikitta's neighbour. Like I said before, I'm not sure how she could have slept through any sort of commotion but it could be argued that some people sleep more deeply than others, so there was nothing conclusive to suggest when it had actually started sounding. It was a real grey area.

The firefighters did decide that the fire would have torn through the bedroom fairly rapidly. The television in the room had melted but the clothing on the radiators, although charred, remained intact. This suggested that the seat of the fire had been somewhere near the television. Although this didn't prove much, it was consistent with the idea that the fire had been started deliberately.

Still drunk and high on cocaine, Whant agreed to drop Ryan and Daniel home a few hours later. It's impossible to tell what was going through his mind as he got behind the wheel and returned to the scene of the crime. We were already there, deranged with worry, but his expression remained blank throughout.

Later that day, he calmly made his way into the centre of

Newport to meet his girlfriend. His biggest concern was not that he'd killed our daughter, granddaughter and beloved pet in cold blood but that his girlfriend 'had the hump' with him for staying out all night. To a casual observer, they were like any other young couple, rowing on a Saturday afternoon as they trailed round the shops. He'd got carried away drinking with his mates, she'd been left at home with the kids and she wasn't happy about it.

Like most couples, they huffed and puffed for a few hours before making up and going home. But later that evening, his girlfriend – Rachel, we later discovered her name was – noticed something untoward.

'You have scratch marks on your arm,' she noted, 'loads of them. What did you get up to last night?'

Whant barely flinched. In a split second, he'd come up with the story about how he'd rowed with an Asian man in the pub. He'd got the scratches, he claimed, when a woman had grabbed him in an attempt to stop them scrapping.

Rachel bought the story – temporarily, at least. Whant was an ex-nightclub bouncer and he could be argumentative when he'd been drinking and taking drugs. It was hardly an unlikely scenario. The police, however, weren't so sure his version of events stacked up.

They started by looking at CCTV footage in the pubs Whant had visited with Ryan and Daniel. There were no leads. They spotted Whant but he hadn't appeared to argue with anyone. There was no Asian male and no woman trying to split them up. DCS Ronayne told them to widen the search. They recovered CCTV footage from 250 premises in the centre of Newport. It was a huge task but they had to exhaust every possible avenue and check every location that Whant could have possibly visited. He'd been drinking heavily, after all, so maybe he'd got the name of the pub mixed up.

But still they found nothing. They appealed for witnesses – maybe the Asian male would come forward. Or perhaps the woman who'd tried to split them up would remember the supposed altercation and contact the police. They received no calls on the matter.

It wasn't definitive proof, of course, but it was the best the officers could manage under the circumstances and DCS Ronyane was quietly confident that they could prove, on the balance of probabilities, that there was no remonstration in the pub.

Which left only one real possibility: that he'd got the scratches when he'd attacked Nikitta and she had tried to ward him off. She would have fought for her life with every fibre of her being and she would never have given up as long as there was a chance she could protect Kelsey-May. Even now, I can hardly bear to think of it. Could any mother?

Sometimes, in my darker moments, my mind wanders to the next part. There are only two people who really know the true sequence of events: Whant and Nikitta. Nikitta is no longer here and Whant will never tell the truth, so the brutality has been left to our imaginations. This is nothing short of sheer torture, as there are a million and one different scenarios that still run through my head on a daily basis. Often I wake up thinking about it and it's usually my last thought before I close my eyes at night. I can see his bulky frame towering over my daughter and her baby bump, the knife in his hand. She didn't stand a chance.

As for the knife, the police immediately set out to find it. They recovered seventy knives from various locations across Newport. None of them had traces of Nikitta's blood on them. Then a large knife was found on the road outside the home Whant shared with Rachel. They DNA tested it and found a partial profile, which they believed to be Nikitta's. It wasn't definitive but it was better than nothing.

The officers had worked around the clock and pre-empted almost everything the defence might throw at them. They were increasingly convinced that Whant's case would be going to trial. He had been remanded in custody, but even in the face of all the evidence they had gathered, he was refusing to admit his guilt.

Chapter Twelve

Limbo

*A*fter the funeral, all we could do was wait for the trial and pray the monster who took our girls from us would be locked away, unable to harm another innocent young woman. Early on, Ian Hodgkinson told us the trial could be months away – it could even take a year. The thought of months of uncertainty stretching out in front of us – an agonising limbo – was almost too much to bear. I didn't know how any of us would get through it.

The torment of waiting for justice was nothing compared to the hell of living without Nikitta. Every day, around 4pm, I'd instinctively listen out for Missy's footsteps and for her paws scratching at the front door. Of course, I was met with deafening silence, which made me break out in a cold sweat.

More than anything, I was consumed by a desire to hold

Nikitta in my arms. When I cradled her badly burned body through the cloth in the mortuary, I couldn't accept that it was the last time I'd ever touch her. There were nights when I was so delirious with grief that I'd go upstairs, tears streaking my face, and roll up a towel from the bathroom. I'd hold it to me, as tightly as I possibly could, until my knuckles were white with the effort. I closed my eyes and begged my brain to switch off for just a second, to allow myself to believe I was cwtching Nikitta instead.

It was no use. I'd open my eyes, throw the towel on the floor and burst into fresh, raw tears.

I was also overwhelmed by the most incredible feelings of guilt. I was so wrapped up in my own pain that it felt almost disrespectful. How could I think of myself when Nikitta never had the chance to hold her baby in her arms? But all I could do was focus on my own sense of loss.

I wrote in my diary.

I feel selfish. I must be honest but every day I think about how I should be a nanna and I should be babysitting. I should have you at the door or at the other end of the phone, asking our advice about Kelsey-May, giving you a rest to go shopping or for you to have a sleep because you're tired. I know I moaned, Keeta, but you know I love you, don't you? And you know even though your Dad said, 'Don't bloody expect us to babysit,' he never meant it. We were all so looking forward to having an extended family, sweetheart. I so miss that opportunity. I love you darlings and miss you so much. I wish I could change what has happened. Love you always and forever xxx.

Every morning, as the spring sunlight slowly crept through the windows, I'd open my eyes and, for just a fraction of a second, everything was as it should be. I'd expect to get ready for work, before coming home to find Nikitta and Missy – and perhaps now Kelsey-May too – outside. Then reality would hit me like a ton of bricks and I'd want to pull the covers over my head and shut out the world.

I had to get up though, or I'd have spent the rest of my days lying in bed, waiting to die myself. For one, we had to make sure Luke was OK, though Patrick and Cheryl were always on hand to look after him when we were having a black day – which was often. Secondly, I knew Nikitta would have wanted us to carry on as best we could.

One of the first things I decided I wanted to do was buy some presents for Claire, the nurse from the mortuary. She'd been so caring and understanding and she'd let me come back for another visit, so I could give them the new clothes for Kelsey-May and hold my girls one last time.

Paul and I decided we wanted to buy some new Moses baskets for the mortuary. The staff there had made the best of what they had but seeing Kelsey-May for the first time in that grotty old thing had made me want to vomit. Money was really tight, as neither of us could bear to go back to work yet, but this was something we really wanted to do. We picked out a beautiful pink Moses basket for a girl and a lovely blue one for a boy. We hoped no other parents – or grandparents – would have to stand in that room and face what we'd had to face but if they did, we wanted to help ease the pain as much as we possibly could.

We took the Moses baskets to Cardiff, along with some flowers, chocolates and a card for Claire. When we gave her the presents, she started to cry.

'I'm sorry,' she said, dabbing her eyes. 'I'm just so touched that you would do this.'

'It's the least we can do,' I replied. 'It's so awful to come in here and see a child lying there like that. We want to do anything we can to make it a bit better for parents.'

Claire's expression held a sad smile. 'We really appreciate you thinking of us at a time like this. I've been doing this job for a long time but this has really got to me, this case.'

It must have been impossible not to be shocked and horrified by the case, no matter how many gruesome sights you may have seen throughout your career. My mind flashed back to the first time we'd been in the mortuary with the FLOs and how they'd choked back tears too.

Shortly after we visited the mortuary, we decided it was time for Luke to go back to school. It had been almost two months since the fire and Paul and I both felt strongly that he needed a bit of normality and routine in his life; to be around his friends. Things were hard enough for him and we didn't want him to spend all day every day brooding over what had happened. Needless to say, we also didn't want his education to be disrupted any more than it already had been.

'Are you and Dad going back to work, Mum?' he asked innocently, when we discussed it with him.

I bit my lip as I felt the tears spring to my eyes. How could I possibly step back into a classroom and listen to the sound of children's laughter? How could I concentrate on numbers or the alphabet for more than a few seconds? I wasn't ready to be Miss Grender again; to pull on that mask and face my little class. Children were so naive. What if they asked an innocent question that made me burst into tears? But then I felt that familiar stab of guilt: I was making Luke go back to school but I couldn't quite manage it myself.

'Yes,' I said, without thinking. 'Yes, we're going back to work too. School will be fine once you're there, love.'

It was a white lie. Now I know we did make the right decision sending Luke back to school. He seemed more at ease being back among his friends and doing normal teenage things, although I imagined his life would never truly be normal again. But it didn't stop me questioning myself and that made me curse Whant over and over again. If he hadn't been so senseless – so evil – Paul and I would still be at work, Luke would never have taken any time off school, our lives would be rolling along as normal and I'd be able to hold Nikitta and Kelsey-May in my arms like I ached to do.

I didn't just want to hold Nikitta, though – I wanted to talk to her too. I longed for mundane conversations about what she was cooking for tea, or who she'd got talking to as she wandered around Broadmead Park with Missy. In turn, I wanted to tell her about the funny things the children at school had said, or pass on some gossip from my workmates. Sometimes I'd find myself speaking to one of the many photographs I had of her in my room. As I spoke, however, my thoughts always became dark.

Sweetheart, I sit and look at your photograph and say the same things. It's so hard, holding a conversation with a photo, sweetheart. So hard.

I just said to Dad, I feel really guilty going out! I just don't want to leave you both home alone. It really hurts me.

Every time I go out, I kiss you both and think about the last time you were alone. How scared you must have been, trying to protect yourself, your body, Missy... how were you feeling? It kills me. I can't imagine the full extent of it, Keeta, but I try to – to make it that bit easier for you. I know that sounds stupid. I know it doesn't help, or make matters easier, especially for me. It hurts me like hell. It's not making anything easier! I don't know why I put myself through it because, deep down, I know it doesn't actually make matters easier for you, sweetheart.

I'm so sorry. Why didn't you come back here that night? I hope it wasn't my fault. If it was, you should have ignored me like you always used to do. Why, Keet? Why?

Love you lots, beautiful girls. Our little angels. Love you xxx

The simplest things could set me off. One morning, I decided to make bacon-and-egg rolls for Paul and me. As I was cooking, the smell nearly knocked me sideways. It reminded me of all those Saturday mornings when Nikitta would come round with Missy in tow, and sometimes Ryan too, hungry for the fry-up they knew we'd be making. I used to love the smell of eggs and bacon; it was so comforting. It reminded me of cosy Saturday mornings, spent laughing and joking with family around me. Now, it made me retch. The only Saturday morning I could think of was the day Nikitta had been taken from us and it would define all of our Saturday mornings from now on. She'd never sit on the couch, balancing her plate on her lap as she tucked into her bacon, Missy running wild at her feet.

Somehow I composed myself and scooped the food into two rolls and piled them onto plates. As I gave Paul his, I could hardly look at him. I took one bite of mine and it stuck in my throat. I tried to have another and swallowed hard. It took every effort to get it to go down and the taste – a taste I'd once loved – almost made me gag. I pushed the roll around my plate for a few more minutes, then threw it in the bin and went upstairs to find my diary.

I wrote,

I hate Saturdays! Because you would spend the whole day with us after having your cooked breakfast. Sundays? I hate Sundays too, because you should be up with us, having your cooked dinner with Nanna and I urging you to eat your greens so Kelsey-May could benefit from them as well as you.

I can't stand cooking bacon, and I can't stand eating

it, because I know how much you liked it. So I binned my roll, went upstairs and cried.

I wasn't allowed to hold my baby girl one last time – not properly. Every parent has a right to hold their child! But you were taken cruelly, sweetheart, taking away our rights to our child. I can't get rid of the constant ache in my throat, heart and pit of my stomach. I'm thinking horrible thoughts! None of this is normal. It's not right! I'm sorry Keeta and Kelsey-May – I don't want to unsettle you all. All I want in life is for my family to be complete and happy – but we're not...

Then something happened which lifted our spirits a little. A local businessman called Dave contacted us through the police, asking if he could get in touch with us. At first I was wary – what use could we be to him? Still, curiosity got the better of me and I called the number I'd been given. We exchanged a few formalities before he cut to the chase.

'Marcia, I hope you don't mind me suggesting this,' he said. 'But my wife and I would like to settle the bill for Nikitta's funeral.'

I was so shocked that I hung up. I don't know what poor Dave must have been thinking! I just stood there with the phone in my hand, shaking slightly, unable to comprehend what he'd said. Although Paul had agreed to pay for the funeral in instalments, money was tighter than ever because neither of us had gone back to work yet. We were behind on bills and the council was chasing us, as we weren't able to pay our rent. It was a catch-22 situation – had we both been unemployed, we'd have been entitled to housing benefit and we wouldn't have had to worry. However, neither of us wanted to quit our jobs because the thought of starting from scratch when we were able to work again was unbearable. Neither of us could have gone through the rigour of interviews and application forms, or the nudges and whispers of new colleagues as they slowly realised who we were.

I suppose I just couldn't believe that a stranger could be so generous. I couldn't find it within me to call him back, so Uncle Paul did it for me.

'What a lovely bloke,' he said, as he rang off. 'He wants to pay for the lot.'

From that moment on, Dave and his wife Jayne became firm friends of ours. Sometimes I think they are our guardian angels. They came along when we needed them most and they've been such a huge support ever since.

Mother's Day was so hard. I had been so looking forward to taking Kelsey-May out and buying her a card to give to Nikitta. Of course, she wouldn't have had a clue what was going on but I'd already planned it in my head, as I knew how much it would have meant to Nikitta. In the end, I still bought the card – but I laid it by the headstone in the graveyard instead.

'You would have been such a beautiful mum,' I said, as I sobbed and placed the card down on the ground. 'So we've got you a card from your beautiful Kelsey-May.'

As I wiped away my tears, I thought about all the big occasions – birthdays, Christmases, anniversaries – stretching out in front of me. Happy family events that should all have been so full of joy. Now they seemed pointless. I never wanted to have another birthday or celebrate another Christmas again. Without Nikitta, what was the point?

I found myself wondering if there really was a God and if he was up there somewhere, could I make a pact with him? Could I trade every birthday, every Christmas, every Mother's Day, and get my girls back? I promised I'd never ask for another present again because nothing anyone could give me would mean anything.

Things were even worse a few weeks later, on Easter Sunday. Ryan came round and got upset. I did feel sorry for him but I had to leave the room; I couldn't deal with anyone else's grief because my own was so overwhelming. Nikitta didn't really like chocolate, so we'd always given her £20 in a card at Easter instead. I just knew she'd have spent it on Kelsey-May. I also found myself daydreaming about what I'd have bought my little granddaughter. She'd have been too young to eat an Easter egg, so I'd have bought her a beautiful soft-toy Easter bunny or chicken, or maybe a nice little dress.

We should have had a house full of love and laughter but it was eerily quiet. Luke couldn't cope with the emptiness we all felt, so he went off to Patrick and Cheryl's. Paul and Ryan had some drinks downstairs but I couldn't bring myself to join them – I didn't want to know what kind of dark places the alcohol would take me. Instead, I went upstairs and wrote in my diary again:

I wish I could cancel Christmas and birthdays. That sounds selfish, I know, but I also know that it is going

to hurt a lot of people not having you both around! I'm
NOT looking forward to it at all. I'm missing you so
much, Keet and Kelsey-May, so, so much. I love you,
baby girls, so much.

When we're sitting in the garden, I feel sick every time
a young girl passes. I feel sick now writing this. I try to
get rid of the feeling by saying something to Dad, but it
just stays on top of my stomach. I don't like feeling like
this, Keet! I want it to stop. My stomach gets so tight
and I don't feel like eating. I just resent seeing young
girls – any teenage girls.

I can't believe what has happened, sweetheart. It's
all so unbelievable, so unreal. Have any of us ever
done anything so wrong that this is how we are being
punished? Why did it happen to you, Keet? I need
answers! We all do. I have never felt scared before, but
I am scared now, it's crazy. You be peaceful, sweetheart,
and cherish being with your daughter forever. Protect
them, Missy. Love you all xxx.

A few weeks later, I decided to go round to the flat again. I
knew it wouldn't be easy – after all, the last time we'd gone,
I'd spent the whole day showering, trying to rid myself of the
smoky smell that made me feel so sick. But I felt I owed it to
Nikitta to salvage what I could of Kelsey-May's.

The man from the council let us in. He was really kind
and he shone his big torch so we could find our way upstairs
to the nursery. The smell was still as pungent as before and I
held my breath the whole way upstairs.

As the nursery door swung open, my stomach clenched violently and I wondered if I might have to run outside and throw up. Paul clasped my hand as the sweat rolled down the back of my neck. The room wasn't as badly damaged by the smoke as Nikitta's room had been but many of Kelsey-May's things were beyond repair. I felt my legs start to go from beneath me as I saw the pink wallpaper we'd so carefully picked out peeling at the edges, blackened by the smoke. The beautiful Moses basket was in the corner of the room, as was the huge pile of nappies Nikitta had been stockpiling. If I hadn't had Paul to cling to, I might have collapsed.

'We need to save everything we can,' I said hoarsely. Paul gripped my hand and nodded silently.

We both stood there for a few seconds before a wave of energy swept over me. I grabbed the bags we'd brought with us and started piling Kelsey-May's outfits into them, one by one. Tears pricked my eyes as I ran my fingers through the gorgeous little dresses and babygros Nikitta had so lovingly picked out but I didn't stop until everything I could salvage was packed away.

We went downstairs and there was a pile of post on the side in the kitchen. We hadn't noticed it the first time we'd called round but Paul picked it up and began to look through it, just in case there was anything important we should take care of.

As he leafed through the letters, his eyes filled with tears and my stomach knotted again, wondering what could be wrong. But then he broke into a sad sort of smile.

'Bloody hell, Marce,' he said. 'She's applied for every loan and credit card going!'

For a split second, anger coursed through me and I ran to snatch the letters from Paul. It was an instinctive thing – I think for a moment I reacted as if she was still alive.

'What the hell?' I said, looking through the letters. 'Her and Ryan – both of them! God, what were they thinking?'

Paul shook his head. 'After everything I told her about debt! Didn't I warn her, Marce, not to take out any credit cards? She'd never have been able to afford this – they'd never have been able to pay all of this back if they'd maxed out these cards. It's thousands! I can't bloody believe these companies would give it to them – that's another thing.'

'I know!' I said. 'It's like it all went in one ear and out the other.'

Suddenly, we fell silent. We'd run out of things to say. After a few seconds, Paul started to laugh and I found the corners of my mouth were twitching too. It was the first time I'd even been close to a smile since the day of the fire.

'You know what,' he said. 'I'm glad she took them out. I'm glad she enjoyed spending their money while she was here. She can't pay it back now, can she?'

I shrugged. 'I suppose she can't.' My eyes travelled to all of the bags on the floor, full of clothes for Kelsey-May. 'No prizes for guessing what she spent it on. Kelsey-May had enough clothes to do her for a year! Maybe more.'

'More, I'd say, by the time you think about all the stuff you bought her!' said Paul. 'Both as bad as each other! Women and shopping, I just don't know!'

We took the bags out to the car and my eyes fell on all of the teddies outside. They were so weather-beaten and dirty now and their colours had faded. But they melted my heart and I just couldn't leave them there. People had given them to Kelsey-May and it just wasn't fair to abandon them.

'Can we take them home?' I asked Paul.

'I'd love to, Marce,' he said, 'but there's so many of them. Will we have room?'

I was defiant. 'We'll find room,' I insisted. 'Come on, help me get them into the car.'

For the next few days, I was a woman on a mission. My washing machine was never off, as I spent hours alternately washing the teddies and Kelsey-May's clothes. They must have all gone through about three loads each – but the clothes still smelled of smoke and the teddies of damp, so I washed them some more.

I didn't know what I wanted to do with them. I don't think I really wanted to do anything with them – I just wanted to have them close to me. We could keep the teddies in the garage and the clothes in the spare room. I just couldn't bear the thought of them being thrown away, or left to fester in a burnt-out house.

As I piled the little outfits into the machine and watched them spinning around inside – flashes of pink, cream and lemon – I thought about Kelsey-May and how it had felt to hold her. She would have been a few months old by then and I imagined her bouncing up and down on my knee. She'd have learned to laugh too and she'd have been gurgling away as I sang my songs to her.

'Look at you two!' Nikitta would have said, laughing. 'You're nuts, Mum!'

I slumped on the floor next to the washing machine. The clothes spinning around had an almost hypnotic effect. It was like I was in a trance, unable to tear my eyes away from all of the dresses my granddaughter would never wear, thinking of all of the memories we'd never make.

In time, Ian was able to tell us that Whant would be appearing at Cardiff Crown Court in July to answer to the charges against him. All he could tell us was that there was significant forensic evidence in favour of the prosecution, which made us think he'd plead guilty.

'I know this sounds a bit stupid,' Paul said, one evening. 'But don't you hope he'll plead not guilty? If he admits it, he won't get as long in jail.'

I nodded. 'I want him locked up for as long as possible. Why should he have it easy?'

'We know he's guilty,' Paul went on. 'Don't we, Marce? So why shouldn't he suffer for as long as possible?'

'Wait a second,' I said. 'If he pleads not guilty, we'll have to sit through the trial and listen to all the details of how she died.' I let out a tiny sob. 'Could you handle that, Paul?'

'I can,' he said, determination in his eyes. 'I can if it means he gets longer in prison.'

'Me too,' I replied, softly. 'We'll just have to get through it.'

Paul locked his fingers through mine and we sat on the couch, staring into space. There were times when I went into a bit of a daze, lost in my own thoughts as I gazed at the wall. Some days, I really wondered what the point in life was. We didn't really have a life any more, just a sad sort of existence.

By now it was May. The woodland behind our back garden was a beautiful and vibrant green and flowers had appeared in lots of our neighbours' gardens. The days were getting sunnier and the nights lighter. The previous year, I'd been so happy as summer approached but now I felt almost angry at nature. How could the seasons keep changing as if nothing had happened?

The sunshine didn't suit my bleak mood. I didn't want to sit in the back garden because I should have been there with Nikitta and Kelsey-May. Every day I thought of Kelsey-May and how she'd be developing. It hurt to think that the tiny baby I'd held in my arms should be trying to sit up on her own and having little bits of proper food. She'd recognise her mum's face and her voice and she'd be outgrowing some of her clothes too. I wondered how she'd be changing physically and what her personality would be like. What would make her laugh and what would make her grumpy?

I've missed you like mad today, Keet. I want you to walk through the door and for me to ask if you want to go shopping with me. I really want to go clothes shopping with you, sweetheart. I want to make you a sandwich and a cup of tea and to look after Kelsey-May so you can have half an hour to yourself. I love you, Keet, so much. I really, really do.

A few weeks later, Jayne and Dave surprised us. They'd booked us a holiday to Tenerife. We didn't tell Luke where we were going until we got to Bristol Airport and he was so overwhelmed that he burst into tears and threw his arms around Jayne. She couldn't help but cry too.

It was a lovely gesture – so unbelievably generous. Jayne and Dave had already gone above and beyond paying for the funeral. Before, we'd have jumped at the chance of a family holiday but needless to say, it just wasn't the same.

We tried our best for Luke's sake but his initial excitement soon faded and he seemed withdrawn and distant. There were so many young girls at our apartment block and sometimes, when I saw a dark-haired girl from behind, my heart would stop for a second as I allowed myself to believe it was Nikitta. But then, as ever, the horrible, gnawing pain in the pit of my stomach would return when she turned round. She wasn't Nikitta, no one was: no one could ever be as beautiful, or special.

It was like we were going through the motions, trying our very best to have a good time when our world had collapsed around us. One afternoon, we went for a walk and I wandered slightly ahead of Paul and Luke, lost in my thoughts. In the window of one shop there was a gorgeous leopard-print dress. Fitted and figure-hugging, it would have looked gorgeous on Nikitta. She'd have been so excited to be wearing trendy little dresses now that she was no longer pregnant. For a moment I stood outside the shop, not daring to go in as I pictured her in it, standing by the mirror, taking a selfie on her phone. I just knew that she would have lost all her baby weight within weeks and she'd be looking a million dollars.

I felt dizzy with grief as Paul caught up with me and placed his hand on the small of my back.

'Let's look in here for a second,' I said.

Tentatively, I walked over to the dress. I picked it up from the rail and ran my fingers across the material.

'Keeta would love that dress,' Paul said.

'I thought that too,' Luke added.

Without another word, I shoved it back on the hanger. Before, I'd have looked at the price tag, weighing up whether or not I could afford to buy it as a little treat for Nikitta, perhaps something to put aside for her birthday or Christmas.

'Let's go,' I said, practically running from the shop.

A few days later, we decided to go to the beach. It was a baking hot day and Paul took Luke to the rocks to look for crabs while I lay on a sun lounger. For a few minutes I closed my eyes but when I opened them, they were drawn to a young couple a few feet away. They had a little girl who looked around eighteen months old and there was an older couple beside them. One big happy family, all giggling away as they focused on this lovely little girl. I pushed my sunglasses down so they wouldn't notice me crying.

I replayed the scene in my head as I wrote in my diary later that night.

I thought of you, and Kelsey-May. You, Kelsey-May and Ryan – of how you'd all be together. You chasing Kelsey-May around the sand, laughing at her, with Ryan

close behind, while Dad, Luke and I sat and watched
you all be a laughing, happy family, and us, the proud
grandparents. I cried.

I miss you SO much, it really hurts my insides. My
heart is truly aching. I love you, sweetheart, and I
can't wait until I see you again. You are so beautiful.
I always told you that, but – this is going to sound
awful, sweetheart – sometimes I think if you weren't so
beautiful, none of this would have happened.

It was far from the first time the thought had occurred to me.
I had always been so proud to have produced such a gorgeous
daughter and I swelled with pride any time people told me
how lovely she looked. I'd celebrated Nikitta's beauty when
she was alive but now that she was dead, I almost cursed
it. Whant had been obsessed with her, driven mad by lust.
Could she have been saved if she hadn't been so stunning?
The unanswered questions were driving me mad.

The next day was my birthday. It was the worst birthday
I've ever had and I've never enjoyed any of my birthdays
since. Even though we were abroad, I got lots of texts from
family and friends. Most of them were lovely but they didn't
make me feel any better because every time my phone beeped
it was a reminder that the one happy birthday message I
really wanted would never arrive. I thought about how
Nikitta would have been so excited to go out and buy me a
card from Kelsey-May and how lovely it would have been to
see the word 'Nan' on the front. She'd have probably bought
me a teddy or a necklace too. Paul tried to make up for it by

sending me a text from his phone signed from Nikitta and Kelsey-May. It was so thoughtful that I burst into tears. It was like he had read my mind.

A few weeks later, it was my turn to be strong, when Father's Day came round. I bought a card to give him from Nikitta and Kelsey-May, but as I wrote it and my tears splashed onto the page, it was my own pain I thought of. I couldn't help it. How I wished we could turn back the clocks.

Chapter Thirteen

Face-to-face with Evil

*C*arl Whant was due in court on 4 July 2011 to enter a plea to the charges against him. It was a Monday and we'd decided to travel to Cardiff Crown Court with lots of family and friends. There would be strength in numbers, we felt.

When he'd first appeared in court, in Caerphilly, just shortly after the fire, I'd decided not to go. I had barely been able to summon the strength to get out of bed, never mind sit in the same room as the man who had torn our lives apart. But this time it was different: I wanted to look him in the eye and force him to see the pain in my own eyes.

A few days beforehand, Ian visited to brief us on what was likely to happen in court. Although we knew the charges he'd be answering to – murder, rape, arson and child destruction – we'd been forced to keep what little else we knew to ourselves. We hadn't even been allowed to share the details with our parents, so they didn't know there was any forensic evidence. It was excruciating. We'd have given anything to be able to break this news gently to all of the people who loved Nikitta as much as we did, but if we'd done this, we'd have risked prejudicing the case. Justice for our beautiful daughter was our number-one priority, so we had no choice but to remain silent.

Not that we knew much ourselves. We still didn't even know the exact cause of Nikitta's death, where her wounds were, or how she'd got them.

Ian also told us that he could advise us how Whant was going to plead, in the strictest confidence. Again, we'd have to keep this from everyone close to us but Paul and I still wanted to know; we had to be prepared.

'He's denying all of the charges,' Ian said. 'He's going to plead not guilty.'

Even though Paul and I had agreed we'd rather sit through a trial and see him jailed for longer than have him admit it and be released early, it was still a massive shock and for a few seconds we were both stunned into silence. I don't think I ever imagined that he would be stupid enough to plead not guilty, as we knew about the forensic evidence that linked him to the crime, even though we didn't know exactly what it was.

'So he's trying to say he didn't do it?' I eventually asked.

'Yes,' said Ian.

'I'm gobsmacked,' I replied. 'I really am.'

'But remember what we said, Marce,' Paul chipped in. He

wrapped his arm around my shoulder. 'This means he'll get longer. This is good for us.'

I threaded my fingers through his as I bit down on my bottom lip. 'I know,' I said. 'I know. I'm just a bit shocked, hearing it out loud. I didn't think he'd be so bloody brazen as to pretend he hadn't done it.'

'I know,' said Paul. 'But we've got to keep positive. This will be worth it if he's locked up for longer. We can get through it. Think how much support we have around us.'

He was right. The trial would be unbearable but we'd just have to find a way of sitting through it. That night, though, I tossed and turned as I thought about all of the horrific things we'd hear when the trial began. Could I cope with listening to how this monster had violated my precious daughter then killed her and our granddaughter in the most senseless and evil way? What would I feel like, sitting in the courtroom, hearing how he callously lit a match and watched as the flat erupted into flames, denying us the chance to see our daughter one last time? What would any mother feel like, in my position?

In the end, I just had to get out of bed and smoke a cigarette. As I opened the window, blowing circles of smoke into the street below, dawn was starting to break. I'd have to do this, for Nikitta's sake. But it was going to be bloody hard.

I couldn't get back to sleep, so I took out my diary and began to write:

I so want to turn back the clock, sweetheart. Everybody does, I know. But you were my female companion, my own flesh and blood, and Kelsey-May would have made us a trio. I was so looking forward to us doing things together and battling against the men! I love you all so much, sweethearts – our two special ladies, and Missy Moo xxx.

A few days later, Ian picked us up and we drove to Cardiff Crown Court for the hearing. A huge, imposing building in the centre of the city, it looked more like a palace than a court, with its spire and rows of columns. As we walked from the car to the court steps, I could feel people buzzing around me, reporters and photographers jostling for the best position as we made our way into the building. The cameras weren't allowed beyond the front door, so they wanted to get a picture of us walking in. I could feel the heat of the flashbulbs on my face and hear the clicking of the cameras but it was like it was happening to someone else; I was just so numb.

I'd never been inside a court building in my life and that in itself was daunting: lawyers rushing around in robes, juggling files and mobile phones; police officers standing by the door, just in case something kicked off; and shifty-looking characters hanging around the corridors in ill-fitting suits as they waited for their cases to be called. The smell of polish and the sense of foreboding grew stronger with every corner we turned.

We were taken to one of the bigger rooms in the building.

It was absolutely huge. I could feel the sweat running down the back of my neck as I held onto Paul's hand.

'We're going to seat you in the viewing gallery upstairs,' said Ian. 'Is that OK?'

I nodded, silently. Paul and I took our seats at the front and our friends and family slowly filtered in behind us. Ryan came separately, with Kerry and Paul, the FLO who had come to the mortuary. No one really spoke but it seemed like an eternity before Whant was brought up from the cells.

I'd tried to imagine what this moment would feel like, seeing the man who had ruined my life. He was in handcuffs and flanked by two guards from the security firm charged with bringing him to the court from prison. I only saw his face briefly, as he was escorted to the dock, but that was enough.

A jolt of pure hatred shot through me. It's hard to describe how it feels to despise another human being so completely but in that moment, all I could think about was what I would do if we were in a room together alone. I imagined what the courtroom would look like if it was completely empty – no police officers or security guards, no lawyers and no reporters filing in with their notepads in their hands, pens poised: no one to witness anything – just us.

I imagined my friends and family had all gone too and even that Paul was no longer by my side. I thought of how I would do it. I'd run down to the dock, taking the steps two at a time. The anger and loathing would be rising in my chest, ready to bubble over at any given moment. I'd tear down the aisle, screaming the word bastard as I ran towards him. My cries would reverberate around the empty room, my hoarse voice echoing. When I got to him, I'd start kicking him, punching him, doing anything I could to make him feel a fraction of the pain he'd inflicted on my daughter.

But as I gazed at the back of his head from afar, I knew I could never do that. I'd have to be content with sitting silently, my hands folded in frustration, praying justice would be done. We'd already been warned to be on our best behaviour – if any of us so much as spoke during the proceedings, we'd all be out. We had to be respectful of the court process or we risked failing to get justice.

The plea would be heard by the Recorder of Cardiff, Nicholas Cooke QC. He was wearing a wig, just like judges do in TV shows, and we all had to stand in silence as he marched to the bench. It felt like we were part of some ridiculous crime drama. I never imagined I'd be a part of something like this in my life.

The hearing took only a few minutes. Whant confirmed his name and that he was of no fixed abode and then the charges were read out to him.

I was still looking at the back of his head, gritting my teeth and sucking my cheeks in as I gripped Paul's hand so tightly my fingers hurt. The horrible, ever present gnawing pain in my stomach was stronger than ever. I felt my insides twist as the judge said the words 'murder, rape, child destruction and arson.' Just one of those crimes would have been unthinkable. To commit all four in the same night was a whole new level of evil.

It was then that I emerged from my daze to hear sobs

ringing out around me. I think my Mum was dabbing her eyes with a tissue and a few people had turned white, while others cradled their heads in their hands. Hearing the charges out loud made everything seem so much more awful.

Mr Cooke confirmed that Whant would be remanded in custody before a trial date was set for early in the New Year. I thought instantly of Kelsey-May. By that point, we'd have been excitedly planning her first birthday. Instead, we'd be sitting through the trial of the man who'd killed her before she'd even been born.

Then one of the lawyers representing Whant got up to speak. He prattled on for a few minutes about how the trial should be held in Cardiff because there was too much ill feeling towards Whant in Newport. At one point, he even tried to get it moved to Bristol! We were livid, as it was so important to us that the trial be held close to home. We didn't mind coming to Cardiff for one morning but the journey would be draining every day for weeks on end. Plus, it meant so much to us that so many of our family and friends wanted to come and support us. Had the trial been moved, many of them wouldn't have had the time or the money to travel miles every day. Thankfully, Mr Cooke stood firm and it was confirmed that the case would be held in Newport.

'Do you think he'll ever admit to what he has done?' I asked Paul later that evening when we got home.

'Never,' he replied. 'It's all one big sick game to him.'

That evening, Ryan and a few of Paul's friends came round for drinks. Increasingly, they were finding comfort at the bottom of a vodka bottle. Without any real structure to their day, Ryan and Paul would often sit in the living room, drowning their sorrows until the early hours. Meanwhile I would sit upstairs alone; I was never tempted to join in. I suppose everyone has different ways of trying to cope with things and this was how they were dealing with it.

Most of the time I just wanted to be alone. I knew Paul relied on his friends and he needed the company and support, so I didn't resent them being in the living room – but most of the time I just wanted to be alone with my thoughts; my private memories of Nikitta that belonged to me and no one else.

The night after the hearing was no different. As the men gathered downstairs, I retreated to my room with my dark thoughts. There were times when the pain was so much that I just wanted to close my eyes and for it all to be over. If Nikitta had been my only child, I dread to think what I might have contemplated. Knowing how much Luke needed me was often the only thing that kept me going.

As I lay on top of the bed, my stomach still churning from the day's events, I felt like I was in genuine, physical pain. I wondered if I'd ever feel like living again. It didn't seem likely.

Feeling the urge for a cigarette, I opened the window and took out my lighter. But as I heard the sound of laughter coming from the living room, my whole body tensed. How could anyone be laughing at a time like this?

It continued, off and on, for about half an hour. Each time I heard a chuckle, rage would course through my veins. I had to stop myself from running downstairs and screaming at them all to shut up and show some respect but I couldn't face looking at anyone who thought it was appropriate to laugh when my daughter was dead. I was mad at Paul for letting all of them into the house.

Eventually, I needed a glass of water, so I traipsed downstairs, stony-faced.

'Hey, Marce,' Paul said. 'You OK, love?' Ryan was standing by the door, gazing at a collage of family photos we'd made. There were some beautiful pictures of Nikitta. 'Ryan, do you want a top-up, mate?'

'Thanks, mate,' Ryan said, nodding.

Paul leaned over to top up Ryan's glass with vodka and I had to inhale sharply.

I gritted my teeth, as I made my way into the kitchen. Realising I wasn't happy, Paul followed me in.

'I'm sorry, Marce,' he said. 'Are we being too loud?'

'It's fine,' I said. My eyes were filling with tears but I didn't want to cry when there were other people in the house. 'Just leave it.'

'I'm sorry,' Paul said, resting his arm on my back. 'It's been a bloody awful day. But we're all talking about Keeta. There are some really funny stories from over the years. Do you remember when—'

'OK,' I snapped, cutting him off. 'OK, OK.'

'It's been lovely to hear people talk and laugh about her,' he went on. 'I'd rather that than no one mentioned her at all.'

'Paul, it's fine,' I said. 'But I'm going to bed.'

I felt really guilty for being angry at Paul. Of course it was nice that everyone was sharing happy memories of Nikitta. I felt horrible for being annoyed at the laughter when they were all reminiscing about good times they'd had with her. It was their way of keeping her memory alive, after all. But I was still a little resentful of the fact they could find some joy in the horrendous situation wc all found ourselves in.

I didn't want to join in; I didn't even want to try. Sharing my precious memories of Nikitta with anyone felt like a crime. I couldn't imagine sitting on the couch, giggling and knocking back vodka, telling everyone about how she used to dress up as Mel C, or how she loved Mr Blobby. It felt wrong – criminal almost – like I was betraying her by sharing our private moments with others. Instead, I confided in my diary.

He won't admit to what he has done because it is too damned disgusting. I hope his stomach churns as much as mine does every day! I hope it churns while he is sleeping! I hope he wakes up through the night and punches his head like I do to get rid of some of the thoughts.

Some people burst into tears today when the charges were read out. We don't think he had family there today. We hope they have all turned against the fucking sicko!

I have loads of memories, sweetheart, loads of really good memories – but I keep them to myself. If I share them, I will cry, because they will no longer be my things to think about. I'll be sharing them and I want to keep them for myself. I just can't speak out loud.

It was horrible today, sweetheart, hearing a stranger reading out loud to us what that monster did to you all. It hit me for six again.

I look fine and dandy on the outside, but my insides feel as though they've been ripped out again. I'm holding on strong to my memories though, sweetheart. No one will stop me smiling about them. No one. I love you, Keeta, so much. I say it every time I write to you, but I really do. And you, Kelsey-May. As far as I'm concerned, I knew you. You were with us for eight months, growing in your mummy's tummy. Keet, I knew her and loved her and miss her as much as you, sweetheart xxx.'

Chapter Fourteen

Waiting Game

*I*n a bid to reintroduce a shred of normality to my life, I tried to go back to work. We were eventually told the trial was scheduled for mid-January so the thought of months of sitting staring at the walls, with nothing to fill my days, filled me with dread. Plus, we needed the money.

I've always said I'm two different people: Marcia at home and Miss Grender at work. To stand in front of a class of children, you need to have a mask that doesn't slip. You can't waver or show any emotion because even young children will sense some weakness and start to play up. When I'm Miss Grender, I'm completely in control. But I hadn't been able to find Miss Grender for a long time and I knew Marcia wasn't up to dealing with nearly thirty hyperactive five-year-olds. I would have to dig deep to find my alter ego.

Children are naturally curious and a few asked me some

innocent questions but others were more malicious. I like to think I'm a good judge of character and even with people at a young age, I can sense the difference. One little girl – we'll call her Robyn – kept asking me about Nikitta, despite repeated warnings from her teacher.

'So what was it that happened to your daughter, Miss Grender?' she asked. 'Is she not here anymore?'

Incredibly, my facade didn't slip.

'You know what happened, Robyn,' I said. My voice was stern but I showed no emotion. 'And you're not to ask me again. I do not want to repeat myself.'

There were days when I couldn't find Miss Grender though, no matter how hard I tried. I'd wake up with tears streaking my face and my heart hammering in my throat, drenched in sweat by another nightmare about the final hours of Nikitta's life and what happened in those awful last minutes. Granted, we knew there was forensic evidence implicating Carl Whant but that was it. My imagination was free to run riot, to play out a million and one different scenarios, each one more awful than the last. Until the trial, I had no way of knowing which was closest to the truth. One of the things I thought about most was the fire. I didn't know if Nikitta had perished in the flames or if she'd died before the fire had been lit. I couldn't cope with the idea of her dying a slow, painful death as she was overcome by the flames. On those mornings, I had no choice but to phone my boss and tell her I couldn't come in.

'I'm so sorry,' I'd say. 'It's Marcia, today. I can't find Miss Grender.'

Luckily, the school were really understanding. Paul wasn't quite ready to go back to work, though, and I was glad he didn't rush back. His job involved long hours on the road and could be really lonely, giving him lots of time to mull things over. I didn't like the idea of him getting upset while behind the wheel. In fact, if I'd had my way, I'd have wrapped him and Luke in cotton wool and never let them leave the house again, just to make sure they were safe. Now the world seemed a far more dangerous place than it had a few months previously.

I was blessed to work with a lovely group of people but it was still really hard to know that my private life was now so public. I'd always been friendly with everyone but I'd only truly open up once I got to know them. Now it was like we were public property and it felt like a massive invasion.

Being around children all day at school could be really hard because, of course, I thought of Kelsey-May and the milestones she'd never meet. She'd never be old enough to go to school and get her hands messy by painting and drawing like the little kids in my class. I thought about how proud Nikitta would have been on her first day in reception class and how she'd have taken hundreds of photos at the school gates.

But this was nothing compared to being around newborn babies. At the end of the summer, a family friend had a little girl. I knew I had to visit, to take round a present and get it over with, but it just seemed so unfair. They could all hold their lovely little girl but we'd had to bury ours.

'You'll feel better once you've gone,' Paul said. 'Maybe best to get it over with.'

He was right. I couldn't avoid babies forever, so with a heavy heart I arranged to pop round. When I walked in and saw her sleeping contentedly in her mum's arms, my heart skipped a beat and my stomach somersaulted. The baby was beautiful, of course, and her mum was glowing but the injustice of it all made my throat tighten. I was happy for them, don't get me wrong, but it was just so hard to deal with.

There were a few other people in the house and the baby was being passed around. I knew it would be my turn to hold her soon and I wasn't sure if I wanted to. I've always adored children but it just felt wrong. I imagined Nikitta looking down on me and I was struck by the most debilitating feeling of guilt. What if she was aghast at me holding another baby? Would she think it disrespectful to Kelsey-May? I swallowed hard.

'Would you like a cuddle, Marce?' my friend asked when the baby had been round everyone but me. She sounded a little on edge, so I spoke quickly and nodded.

'Yes, please,' I answered.

It was an awkward situation and I did feel for the other people in the room. It would have been rude to exclude me and it would have just made things even tenser. But to hand me a tiny baby girl knowing I couldn't hold my own granddaughter in my arms was a minefield too.

The pink bundle was passed to me and I stroked the fine covering of hair on her little head. She was gorgeous and it felt lovely to have a baby in my arms but I didn't feel tempted to pretend I was holding Kelsey-May. This baby, lovely as she was, would never be as special to me as Kelsey-May and it was foolish to pretend otherwise. A wave of nausea swept over me and I had to breathe deeply to stop the bile rising in my throat. After a few minutes, I handed her back and made my excuses.

When I got home that evening, I felt suffocated by guilt. I could barely bring myself to look at all of the beautiful pictures of Nikitta in the living room and I had to turn my back on her collage because it hurt too much. How could I hold another baby in my arms when Kelsey-May was gone? I told myself it was all my fault; if I had never given birth to Nikitta, none of this would have happened.

It's all so sad, heart-wrenching, unbelievable. I love all of the photos of you in the living room but I can't handle looking at them all the time, it's too heartbreaking. I want them hanging in the house, of course I do, but maybe not as many as we have got in the living room. I hope you understand what I'm saying and feeling, sweetheart. I love you and see all of your faces every single day and always will until the day I die.

I brought you into this sick, twisted world and I hate myself for that. You probably do too. If you do, sweetheart, I wouldn't blame you at all. I'm sorry.

If we did something wrong when we were little, my Nan used to say: 'God will pay you back in many different ways.' I once stole 20p from your Nanna's purse when I was in the juniors to buy chocolate bars, and another time I stole nappies for a friend that had a baby and no money. If any of those things are why I'm being punished, why the hell are you getting the punishment? Why not me? I tried to right the wrongs in so many different ways when I was younger and growing up, even to this day but none of it mattered. Why my family? Why not me?

I can't see the future anymore. I've tried – but I can't. I miss you all so, so, so much and love you immensely. I am so empty it's unbelievable. All I want to do is wrap Luke and Dad up and either lock them up to keep them safe or send them to a better place where nothing or no one can hurt them or take them away.

I can't stop ringing you in work and there's no answer! I'll keep trying, though.

Hold each other tight, sweethearts. Loads of hugs and love and loads of kisses xxx.

Work was even harder as Christmas approached and the children began to prepare for their parties and concerts. I wished it were possible to cancel Christmas forever. I'd always looked forward to it so much in years gone by, especially when Nikitta and Luke were little. By rights, we should have been enjoying Kelsey-May's first Christmas.

Everywhere I went, people were talking about the festive season, even as early as November. I'd overhear the girls at work chatting about who was doing Christmas dinner this year and what they were buying for their kids and my stomach would knot.

'This is going to be the best Christmas ever!' one of them

said gleefully while I was still in earshot. Of course, she hadn't said it to me directly but I still felt consumed with rage. She hadn't meant any harm but I would never have a happy Christmas ever again and woe betide anyone who tried to wish me one.

Before Christmas Day, we had Nikitta and Paul's birthdays to get through. Paul's was a bit of a blur and I don't think he felt much like celebrating. We'd planned to let off some lanterns on Nikitta's birthday and we were all just focused on that. As the lights soared into the sky, I desperately wished I could go with them and sail up beyond the stars. Maybe then we'd all be reunited and I could watch over Luke and Paul from above. At that moment in time, it seemed to be the only release from the pain I was feeling. I couldn't bear it and I couldn't see a way out. Of course, I'd have never done anything stupid – but that didn't mean I didn't think about it.

Before, I'd cursed myself for bringing Nikitta into the world only to be met with such unimaginable suffering but now I was so glad we'd had those nineteen precious years. I couldn't imagine what life would have been like without her. If only I could have her back for one more, I'd lay down my own life.

As I had predicted, Christmas Day was awful. Coming downstairs and seeing just one pile of presents was like being kicked in the stomach repeatedly and I swear I felt actual, physical pain.

I could tell Luke was trying to be brave for me and that broke my heart, as I just wanted to take him in my arms and sob and sob and sob. I almost did when he handed me some perfume. He'd signed the card from Nikitta, Luke, Kelsey-May and Missy.

We went to the graveyard with my parents and Mum broke down. It was all too much for her and I didn't want to crumble too, so I tried my best to keep the tears at bay. Afterwards, Ryan came round and we tried to get through a Christmas dinner of sorts but you could have cut the atmosphere with a knife. There were no crackers, no party hats, no music and certainly no laughter: and all, of course, because there was no Nikitta.

On New Year's Eve, instead of going out to a party, I sat at home, crying into my diary and praying no one would be stupid enough to text me and wish me a happy New Year. As January dawned and 2012 began, the trial was just a few weeks away. Soon, we'd find out every grotesque detail of what had happened to our girls. We needed to know but listening to it would be the hardest thing I'd ever done in my life.

I've never hurt anyone, mentally or physically. Nothing cruel enough to deserve what has happened to us, to you, and poor Kelsey-May and Missy. If there is a God and if He is looking over my shoulder now, ask Him to let me know what I've done. I need to know, Keet! Pass on my message, Keet, sweetheart. I love you and I wish I could take all of this away from everyone.

I'm preparing myself for what I'm going to hear at the trial but I don't think I – we – will ever be prepared. I'm so scared, petrified, sick, nervous, everything! I have a question which I really need an answer to. I asked it once, but it couldn't be answered. I think they should know the answer now. I want – need – to know but I'm so scared of hearing the answer.

How did you die, Keet?

I haven't asked it lately because it's one of those things that sticks in your throat. I find it hard to ask the question out loud. It's torture! I couldn't bear to hear it said out loud in court, in front of everyone because I know I'll break down or go mad that we weren't told privately. I need to know before others know so I can be the stronger one when it is said out loud for all to hear. It's going to be hard, painful, draining, upsetting, unbelievable... God, every emotion going! Help us through, Keet! I know your dad needs it. So do I! Why didn't you stay here that night? Why didn't you try ringing? I think you may have but only your phone can tell us that.

I'll speak to you soon, sweetheart. You give that granddaughter of mine a massive hug and a kiss – Missy too. I'm sending you one right now, through my heart and mind. Sleep tight, girls. Love you now, always and forever xxx.

Chapter Fifteen

Crown Court

*I*an visited us the day before the trial. He told us that, at certain points in the case, he wanted to brief us on what was likely to come up in court the following day, so it wouldn't come as too much of a shock. It went without saying that Paul and I had to treat this information in the strictest confidence.

The first thing he wanted to talk us through was exactly how Nikitta had died. It was the moment I'd been dreading but I was so relieved that we would get to hear the truth within the privacy of our own home and not in the middle of a cold courtroom surrounded by strangers.

As calmly as he could, Ian talked us through the stab wounds. He told us how Nikitta had been stabbed twice – once in the stomach and once in the abdomen. It was strange to think the police had known this for months and we were only getting to hear the results of the post-mortem now, eleven months later, but we understood it was important to keep the case safe.

Ian was as tactful as he could be but there's no easy way to tell someone about how their daughter and granddaughter were stabbed to death.

My head was in my hands and Paul had reached over to cwtch me as I let Ian's words run through my head.

'So she was stabbed in the stomach,' I said slowly. 'And that… and that reached Kelsey-May?'

Ian bowed his head. 'I'm afraid so, Marcia.'

I suppose I had always assumed that Kelsey-May had died because Nikitta had died. Even if there were a chance she could have been delivered safely, she'd never have survived the fire. But, suddenly, I remembered being in the mortuary and how I'd instinctively tried to remove the horrible bonnet they'd put on her head.

I couldn't get enough air in my lungs and I started to hyperventilate. Paul stroked my arm and helped calm me down until, eventually, my breathing slowed to a normal rate.

'So you mean that…' my voice tailed off as I tried to find the words to utter the unthinkable out loud. 'You mean that he…?'

Paul pulled me close to him. 'You're OK, love,' he said. 'You don't have to say it out loud if you don't want to.'

But I had to – otherwise I don't think I would ever have believed someone was capable of something so evil.

'He stabbed her in the stomach – deliberately – so Kelsey-May would die, too?' I said.

'That's for the jury to decide,' he replied. 'But there was a stab wound to Nikitta's stomach. We know this for a fact.'

How much more could we take? I could feel the colour draining from my already ashen face as I tried – and failed – to comprehend how someone could be so evil. He hadn't just destroyed my daughter, he had destroyed everything important to her in one fell swoop: her child, her dog and her home.

'Tell me, Ian,' I went on. 'Tell me, honestly. Was it quick?'

Ian met my eye. 'Yes, Marcia,' he said. 'She would have died almost instantly from the wound to her neck.'

I closed my eyes and for a split second – a fraction of a moment – I allowed myself to feel the tiniest wave of relief. I had been so scared that Nikitta had still been alive when the fire had been lit. In some of my most horrific nightmares, I'd imagined her lying on her bed, badly wounded but conscious, writhing in agony as the flames burned her skin and smoke filled her lungs. I'd been terrified that she'd been so severely injured that she was unable to escape – that she'd died a slow and painful death, life gradually ebbing from her as the fire raged around her. I cried into Paul's shoulder but I didn't want to show my tears, so I dabbed my eyes quickly and sat upright.

'I'm glad it wasn't the fire,' I said, still sobbing. 'I'm just glad she didn't suffer until the very end.'

Later that evening, a young girl walked past the front of our house. She was a little older than Nikitta would have been – maybe twenty-four or twenty-five – and she was heavily pregnant. It was as if someone up there was taunting us, sending her to remind us of what we'd lost on the eve of what would be one of the most difficult days of our lives.

I didn't know this girl who was shuffling past my window, exhausted from the weight of the life she was carrying inside her. I wondered if she had planned her pregnancy or if it had taken her by surprise. Regardless of the circumstances, I thought of how excited and nervous she must be, in the final weeks of her pregnancy, as she waited for this little life to come along and change everything. It sounds so silly but at that moment in time, I missed being pregnant myself. I wanted to feel a little life growing inside me; to experience once more the joy of what two people can create through love. I ached to run outside and touch this stranger's stomach and to feel her baby kicking, impatient to make his or her big entrance into the world, as Kelsey-May would have done.

My heart was pounding in my chest and I could feel tears once more streaming down my face. I ran to the toilet and shut myself inside for a few minutes, convulsing with sobs.

Neither Paul nor I slept well that evening. We tossed around and took turns hanging out of the window, chain-smoking, in a bid to cope with the stress.

'Give us strength, Keet,' I whispered into the darkness. 'Because God knows we're going to need it.'

On the morning of the first day of the trial – 18 January 2012 – Ian picked us up from home and took us to Newport Crown Court. The building wasn't as grand as the court in Cardiff. In fact, I'd walked past it many times while running errands in town but I never imagined I'd have any reason to go there.

The press had already gathered outside when we got there just after 9am. By now I was used to having my photograph taken and it was the least of my concerns. As long as no one tried to approach me, I could deal with the camera lights flashing.

Of course, they were desperate for a picture of Ryan too but he wasn't with us. He was brought to court separately and he wasn't allowed to listen to the first part of the trial. He'd been called as a witness for the prosecution and it was important he didn't hear any of the evidence before taking to the stand. Again, this could have meant that Whant's lawyers had a case to argue their client hadn't had a fair trial.

I felt sick with nerves and hatred at the thought of seeing Whant again but, as I'd stood alone in the living room, gazing out of the window and wondering how I'd cope with what I was about to hear, I made a pact with myself: I wasn't going to cry. Not a single tear would fall from my eyes within the courtroom. Of course, I'd come home at night and shut myself away, crying until my face hurt – but in public, my eyes would remain dry.

I know people will think this sounds crazy. If anyone has the right to break down in court, it's the mother of a murder victim. But all I could think about was the night Whant had come round to our house, clutching his horrible petrol-station flowers and feigning sympathy. He'd been desperate to call round, to see the agony etched on our faces and to see how we were dealing with what he'd done. It was all part of his sick, depraved, twisted little game. Every tear I shed would be a victory for him and I couldn't bear to let him win. He wouldn't break me – of that I was sure. My stubborn streak would just have to see me through this next tortuous month. If people thought I was a hard-faced, emotionless cow, so be it. They'd never know the tears I cried in private but that didn't matter – they didn't need to.

As we'd never been to a big trial before, we didn't realise how fraught with delays everything could be. In the end, proceedings didn't start until 2pm. There was just enough time for Greg Taylor QC, the prosecution lawyer, to give his opening speech. The details, naturally, were horrific.

'Nikitta should have been safe in her own flat,' he said solemnly. 'But someone raped her. Someone murdered her.'

He began to describe Nikitta's injuries. The wound to her neck was 9 cm deep and the wound to her stomach had penetrated Kelsey-May. Paul broke down. I could feel him shaking and sobbing beside me and there were a few muffled cries from other friends and family members. I didn't know how severe the stab wounds had been and I felt like I'd been kicked in the stomach but I was so glad I had been told about them before we'd come to court, otherwise my steely mask might have slipped.

As Paul wiped his eyes, I focused on Whant. He was sitting in the glass dock at the front of court and he looked pathetic. But, just as Mr Taylor began to describe the fire, he turned round and looked straight at me. A violent chill shot through my whole body. He was enjoying this, just as I'd predicted. He was looking for a reaction. This was his sick moment of glory and he was going to lap up every second. It was beyond evil.

I sucked my cheeks in and, with steely determination, I met his gaze. I stared at him, hard, for a few seconds before he turned back round.

Mr Taylor then started to describe the scratch marks on Whant's arms. He explained the excuse the defendant had given to police – that he'd got into a fight with an Asian man in a pub. Mr Taylor said that the prosecution refuted this – they believed the scratches had been caused by Nikitta when she'd tried to defend herself.

This was too much for Paul and his head fell into his hands again. I wished so badly that I could take his pain away. It killed him that he hadn't been there to defend his precious little girl against this monster but how could he have known? How could any of us? Like Mr Taylor said, she should have been safe in her own home but she wasn't.

I grabbed his hand and knotted my fingers through his, squeezing it tightly to comfort him. It was a strange sort of role reversal. Usually I was the one who needed comforting – the one who couldn't stop crying – but now the tables had turned. Seeing Paul so upset was unbearable and his pain hurt me just as much as my own. Perhaps we couldn't both be weak at the same time. One of us had to have some strength, or we'd never survive.

The jury were shown photographs of the fire. Neither Nikitta nor Kelsey-May had stood a chance in hell.

'Bastard,' I muttered under my breath, not loud enough

for anyone to hear. Paul's hand was still entwined with mine and I gripped it so hard my knuckles turned white.

When we went home that night, sleep was impossible. A few friends and family members came back to the house with us and they didn't leave until the early hours. When they'd gone, Paul and I got into bed but we didn't sleep much. We tossed and turned, once more leaning out of the window in rotation to smoke. It was obvious that we'd be running on coffee, nicotine and adrenaline for the next few weeks.

Mr Taylor continued his opening speech the next morning. We heard about the CCTV footage DCS Ronayne and his team had painstakingly gathered, as well as all of the DNA evidence. We'd had no idea just how many hours of work had gone into the case and we were astounded at the level of evidence against Whant. I found myself studying the jury: seven men and five women, ordinary people just like us. The fate of this monster was in their hands. What if they believed his lies and found him not guilty? How would we ever be able to go about our daily lives if he was walking the streets? What if he did it again, to another innocent girl, and someone else's family had to live through this hell? It was too awful to contemplate.

If that wasn't hard enough, we were soon to be dealt another hammer blow. Again, in the interests of a fair trial and securing a safe conviction, Whant had to be presented with all of the evidence the police had gathered against him. Naturally, this included the result of the vaginal swabs used to prove he'd had sex with Nikitta.

At the eleventh hour – just a few weeks before we were due to go to court – he'd come up with an explanation for this. Mr Taylor told the jury that this evidence had not been mentioned in twenty-six previous police interviews – to me, an obvious indication that it was completely fabricated. But, when I heard what his explanation was, I nearly collapsed.

Whant had admitted he'd had sex with Nikitta the night before she died but he'd claimed it was consensual.

As I dug my nails into Paul's hands I was gripped by a compulsion to dive out of the public gallery and put my hands around his neck. Not only had he violated my poor girl in the most brutal way, now he wanted to defile her memory with this filth.

'Ryan called me into the bedroom and I saw he was naked, lying on top of Nikitta, who was also naked,' Mr Taylor said, reading from the statement. 'He invited me to have sex with her. I agreed and proceeded to have consensual sex with her. I did not wear a condom. After sex, I went to the kitchen, where Ryan was ironing his jeans.'

Paul's face was almost purple and I could hear people around us muttering obscenities under their breath but I turned round and shot them all a look. I didn't want the sick bastard to have the satisfaction of knowing he was getting to us. Besides, Ian had warned us to tell our family and friends that we had to be on our best behaviour in court or we wouldn't be allowed to watch the rest of the trial. No matter how emotional we got, we had to keep calm.

Throughout the rest of the day, I kept having hot flushes.

My face burned scarlet and the sweat began to drip down my back. Each time, I would look up to find Whant staring at me, straight in the face.

I knew his game. He was willing me to break down, desperate for me to cry, but he would never beat me. I knew he'd made it all up, thinking he would get away with it, but who in their right mind would truly believe a stunning young woman like Nikitta would willingly have sex with a beast like him? He was on another planet.

I continued to eyeball him, refusing to break eye contact. Eventually, he looked away and swallowed hard. Unbelievably, his legal team later tried to claim we had been intimidating him because *we* kept looking at *him*! It was absolutely outrageous. Ian had a duty to pass their complaints on to us but he knew how angry they would make me.

'*I* am intimidating *him?*' I screeched. 'Well, I think my daughter would have felt pretty bloody intimidated when he broke into her flat in the middle of the night and raped and murdered her! How can his lawyers have the fucking audacity to say this?'

Paul was just as riled up. 'I can't go down there and physically kill him,' he said. 'I've got to sit in the same room as him, every day, for a whole month, knowing what he did to my little girl and I can't lay a finger on him, even though all I want to do is jump down and smash that fucking glass and do to him what he did to Nikitta. Do his fucking stupid lawyers have any bloody idea how that feels? I can't do anything else, so I'll fucking stare at him as much as I want.'

It wouldn't be the first time we felt like we were the ones on trial.

In my diary that night, I wrote,

It's so hard not to cry. But I don't want that scumbag to have the satisfaction of hurting another woman! That is what he wants but NO WAY! If it makes me look like a hardened cow with no feelings, fine. Today, I had a prickly feeling a few times and I was feeling hot. Each time I had this feeling, I looked at that piece of shit behind the glass and he was staring at me. Every time! I couldn't back down, though. You know me, Keet! I think he expected me to cry. In the end he looked away first. I hope he choked on his tongue and shit and pissed himself in the process.

We've got to keep our eyes fixed on the right people and our tongues held still and not say a word. Our family, as Ian has said a number of times, is doing us proud and being so dignified. I smile and say: 'They will carry on being dignified.' In my head, I know it's all a show but we'll have our day and it's coming soon.

The weekend passed in a bit of a blur and before we knew it, it was time to go back to court on the Monday. That day, Nikitta's neighbour, Sarah Voisey, would be giving evidence.

As we filed into the public gallery, taking our usual seats, I noticed a middle-aged woman sitting on the other side of the court on her own, her head bowed. She looked meek and unassuming and I was overcome by a feeling of pity for her, even though I'd never met her. For a few minutes, I couldn't take my eyes off her and so I asked Ian who she was and what she was doing there.

'Oh,' he replied. 'Well, that's his mum.'

'His mum?' I echoed. 'As in him, in the dock?'

There were times when I could barely bring myself to utter Whant's name and this was one of them.

'Yes,' Ian said. 'She's come every day so far.'

When Sarah Voisey took the witness stand, I soon forgot about Whant's mum, though. She was giving evidence via a video link and I was hanging onto her every word. It sounds silly but I'd even taken my diary to court, so I could make some notes on what she'd said. She was the only person who could have heard Whant breaking into the house; the only person who might have had some clue as to what my daughter's last minutes might have been like.

She started by saying that she hadn't been sleeping well because her daughter had been teething. Mr Taylor asked her a few questions and established that she'd fallen asleep around 4am on the morning of Nikitta's death. An hour and a half later, she'd been woken by a faint beeping sound – a sound we now knew to be the fire alarm.

She'd searched her own flat and, unable to establish where the noise was coming from, she went back to bed. The alarm had woken her again an hour later but, when questioned on this, she simply answered that she thought Nikitta and Ryan 'would deal with it.'

When I heard this, I wanted to reach into the screen and give her a good shake. Of course, it wasn't this woman's fault my daughter had died and she couldn't have prevented Whant from doing what he did – no one could. But how could anyone lie in bed and listen to their neighbour's fire alarm sounding for a whole hour without doing anything? Why hadn't she just stuck her head out of the front door to check if they were OK?

I don't think for one second, of course, that she'd have imagined Nikitta was lying dead on the bed. No one expects something so horrific to happen in their own street. But I just wanted to scream with frustration. She'd said before that the sound insulation was so bad that she could hear Ryan and Nikitta walking around upstairs. Nikitta wouldn't have let Whant touch her without a fight. Why didn't she wake up? Why, against all the odds, did she sleep through the commotion? She wouldn't have had to do anything dangerous – just one call to the police and it could have all turned out so differently.

In the end, she didn't call the fire brigade until just before 8am, when her own smoke alarm started to sound.

'My flat was getting really hot and stuffy and I kept hearing this beeping sound,' she said. 'I phoned the fire brigade, who told me to leave and try to knock on my neighbours' door. When I got outside, I could see smoke coming out of the window. I began frantically knocking on the door but got no answer. I kept banging the door for about ten minutes – my knuckles were red and sore.'

It was too late. The damage had been done. A few minutes later, we'd had the call from Ryan's mum Kerry and our world had imploded.

'I just don't understand,' I said to Paul when the jury retired for a break. 'Why couldn't she have woken up? I wish she'd woken up.'

But she hadn't woken up and we couldn't turn back time. It was galling but true.

I went over the details again that night as I wrote in my diary.

She heard the smoke alarm at 5.30am but she didn't do anything about it. The details are so harrowing. It affects everyone here, I know it does, you can tell. It's awful. My head thinks about you every day. My heart bleeds for you. I can't believe it was you, Keet. I wish we could take it all away from you, sweetheart. Love you very much forever and always xxx.

The next day, we went to court again but Ian took us to one side and explained that the pathologist who had conducted Nikitta's post-mortem, Dr Stephen Leadbetter, would be giving evidence. As always, he left the decision up to us but he suggested it might be better if we didn't listen to what he had to say. Already we knew how Nikitta, Kelsey-May and Missy had died. We didn't need to hear it all again, complete with the gruesome, intimate details.

As we left the court, I saw Whant's mum shuffle in, her eyes fixed on the ground. She didn't meet my gaze, or look at any of her friends or family as she walked past us. It sounds silly but I hadn't stopped feeling sorry for her since I'd heard who she was. I wondered what it must feel like for her, having to come here every day and listen to what he'd done. As a mother, I can't imagine I could ever stop loving my children with all my heart, no matter what they'd done. But what happens when you give birth to a monster like him? How must it feel knowing you've brought such evil into the world? I didn't know what kind of upbringing he'd had but it wasn't his mum's fault that he'd done this.

I imagined how I'd feel if I were in her shoes, wondering how a baby I had loved and nurtured could turn out to be so depraved. She must have been feeling really intimidated, watching us sitting with dozens of our friends and family as she cowered there on her own. Did she think he was guilty, I wondered, as she sat there with her hands clasped, staring at the dock. I know that if I had been in her shoes, I'd have wanted nothing more than to believe it had all been a mistake; that I hadn't produced a child who would grow to be so evil. But, as the evidence mounted up against him, surely it must have been starting to dawn on her. Her pain was different from mine. Her child was still alive, sure, but could she ever look at him in the same way again, knowing he'd killed someone?

'Is that his mum?' one of our friends said. 'Hope she's fucking proud of him!'

'Do you think she's OK?' I said. 'I feel a bit sorry for her.'

Everyone turned round and looked at me like I had just suggested flying to the moon for lunch.

'Marce, you're mental!' another friend said. 'Fuck her! Worry about yourself and how you're going to get through this. You've got enough on your plate without worrying about that twat's mum!'

When we went back into court, though, I couldn't help but look at her again. I was gripped by a compulsion to sit down next to her and speak to her, mother to mother. I wanted her to know that I didn't blame her for what her son had done. I guess I also wanted to know if she believed him or if she was just turning up every day out of loyalty. I don't know what I'd have done in her position.

As Ian drove us home that evening, I asked about her.

'Do you think she would speak to me?' I said. 'I really want her to know that I don't think it's her fault.'

Ian shook his head. 'It's not a good idea, Marcia. You can't approach her in court either. You need to just let her be.'

'Couldn't I maybe speak to her after the trial?' I went on, refusing to let it go. 'I'm not going to be angry. I'm not angry at her, just at her son. I just want to find out what she makes of all this. I think it would help.'

Ian shifted uneasily in the driver's seat as he changed gear. 'I can try to find out,' he said. 'But I just don't think it's going to happen. We'd also have to get you a police escort, to make sure she was safe.'

It was so ridiculous that I almost laughed. 'Ian,' I said, 'I'm not the criminal here! I don't want to do her in! Do you think, even if I did, I'd be so stupid as to do it in a building full of judges and police officers?'

'I know, Marcia,' he said. 'I don't think for a second you would do anything to hurt her. It would just be procedure.'

He pulled on the hand brake as we reached the traffic lights. 'I don't think it will be possible. I'll ask but don't expect it to happen.'

The next day at court, Whant's mum shuffled past me more quickly than usual. She wasn't alone, though. This time she'd brought along her sister – his auntie – who threw a filthy look in my direction and exhaled loudly as she walked behind his mum, shaking her head.

'Sorry,' said Paul. 'Is it us on trial now? What is her fucking problem?'

'I've made some inquiries,' Ian told me. 'I'm afraid Mrs Whant won't speak to you. She doesn't want to. She's backing her son all the way, apparently.'

I nodded. 'Thanks for trying. It would be nice if I could hear it from her, though. I just want to know what she's thinking.' I sighed. 'But it's OK, I get it. I can't talk to her.'

For the next few days, we heard lots of the evidence DCS Ronayne and his team had spent months collecting. The reams of CCTV, the examinations involving the car, the DNA found on Whant's clothes and statements from lots of different civilians and police officers who had been involved in the case. It was all so much to take in but I was still making notes on all of the details. I know the police had enlisted the help of lots of experts, who were fantastic at their jobs, but I was terrified something would slip through the net and he'd get off. I thought it best to have everything down on paper, in case I forgot a crucial detail.

It was hard to believe we'd only be going to court for just over a week. Neither Paul nor I could really sleep much – I think I was getting about an hour or so every night if I was lucky. We would head up to bed, exhausted, about 1am and usually we'd fall asleep fairly quickly. Then we'd both spring awake at 3am on the dot, as if our bodies were in sync. We could rarely get back to sleep as our stomachs would start to churn from thinking about the day ahead and the horrors we'd no doubt have to hear. We'd be so stressed out that we'd sit and smoke for the rest of the night, taking it in turns to hang out of the window, waiting for the sun to come up.

One night, towards the end of the second week of the trial, I drifted off to sleep as usual and I started to dream. I was holding Missy and she was yapping away, licking my face. She was wearing a little parka jacket that Nikitta had bought her and she looked really cute. But, as I stroked her fur, she began to disintegrate in my hands. I was screaming, breathless, trying to cling to her fur, but she was ebbing away, falling through my hands. Before I knew it, I was bolt upright in bed, hyperventilating.

'Marce, you're dreaming,' said Paul. 'You're OK, it's just a dream.'

'Oh, Paul,' I said, sobbing, 'it was Missy! I had her here, right here. But now she's gone.'

Paul took me in his arms and stroked my hair as I cried a little more. But instead of reaching for my cigarette packet, I took out my diary.

Hello, sweethearts. I've wanted to write every day but with court going on, my head is blank. When we get home, the only thing I can talk to you about is court

226

and I can't keep doing that. You're probably there listening to it all yourselves anyway.

As you know, so far throughout this case I have been a hard-faced cow. But today, I cried when I got home and I saw your photo by the side of the bed, Keet. I wanted to feel your arms around me, for you to give me a hug. I was remembering a hug from you and wishing I could have one right then. I could feel it in my mind. I really, really love you, Nikitta, and I would do anything to have you here! I'm missing you so much. I don't know what we are going to do. Goodnight, sweethearts. Love you always and forever. Sweet dreams, girls xxx.

Chapter Sixteen

A New Agony

Once Ryan had given his evidence, he would be allowed to sit in the courtroom and watch the rest of the trial with us. He was scheduled to take the stand on Thursday, 2 February. It was almost a year to the day Nikitta had died, but for us, time had stood still.

I was apprehensive about his testimony. I wasn't focused so much on what Ryan was going to say, but on how Whant would react. I knew he'd be loving the drama, turning round to look at me whenever he could, desperate to see what he was doing to me.

If only that had been all I had to worry about.

Ryan looked really nervous when he was called to the stand and I actually felt sorry for him. I was glad neither Paul nor I had to stand up and give evidence – God knows how daunting it would have been. Mr Taylor started off by asking Ryan a little about his relationship with Nikitta – all fairly standard stuff about how they'd met and how long they'd been seeing each other. He then asked about Whant and Ryan explained how he'd been like a brother to him.

'I could speak to him about anything,' he said sadly. 'I was closer to him than I was to any of my friends.' He swallowed hard. 'But Nikitta didn't like him. I think she was jealous I spent a lot of time with him. Sometimes, she wouldn't let him in the flat.'

Kerry was sitting with her hands folded in her lap a few seats along from me. Later she told me that she'd had a gut feeling that Whant had been behind the fire and that she'd even confronted him but he'd denied it. Ryan was staring at his cousin – his former best friend – hatred flickering in his eyes. For once, I got him. I understood how he felt; we were on the same page.

Mr Taylor began to question Ryan about the events of 4 February – the night before Nikitta had been killed. He admitted that he and Whant had planned to go to Tesco to steal some alcohol and I looked at Paul and rolled my eyes as subtly as I could. I didn't want to let Whant see any emotion on my face. Ryan was just young and stupid but this really pissed me off: he should have been at home looking after Nikitta, not out nicking booze from a supermarket.

Mr Taylor then took Ryan through the events of the night. He explained how he and Whant had gone back to Broadmead Park to get changed before watching the rugby. Nikitta hadn't spoken to Whant – she hadn't even said hello or goodbye. Then they'd gone to Kerry's to watch the first half of the rugby before heading to the pub. From there they'd gone to a nightclub and started chatting to the girls who would later invite them back to Corelli Street.

'Some of the group left the club to take cocaine,' Ryan said. I felt my stomach turn. Nikitta had absolutely hated drugs. I'd known Whant was a big cocaine user and I'd always suspected Ryan had dabbled in it too but I'd never had any proof. He bowed his head before adding, 'I was one of them.'

At this point, Whant scribbled something on a piece of paper and passed it to his solicitor. He had this stupid half-grin on his face and he turned round and looked me up and down. I squeezed Paul's hand as tightly as I could underneath the seat. I was really angry. In fact, I was bloody fuming. How dare this little shit leave my pregnant daughter alone in their flat to steal booze and take cocaine! I wanted to walk right up to the witness stand and give him a massive slap. I'd been right all along – he was no good. How the hell had my beautiful daughter ended up with a bloody no-hoper like this?

But I couldn't lose my rag because Whant's eyes were upon me, boring into me, waiting for me to explode with rage and lash out at Ryan. He'd have loved that. He hadn't destroyed us all enough by taking Nikitta away, now he wanted to twist the knife by playing us off against each other, watching us fighting among ourselves. Well, he was severely mistaken if he thought he was going to see a flicker of emotion on my face.

It was hard to keep my cool as Ryan's evidence went on,

especially when he admitted that he and the others had been taking cocaine well into the early hours as they partied in Corelli Street. I felt like someone had kicked me in the gut. It was bad enough that he'd left her alone when she was so close to giving birth but he'd left her alone to do this? What hope would Kelsey-May have had with him as a dad? What a bloody waste of space he was!

Whant's barrister, Christopher Kinch, then began cross-examining Ryan and things got even worse. I didn't know who I was more annoyed at: Ryan or Kinch. The barrister was trying to get Ryan to say he'd invited Whant to have sex with Nikitta and that made me sick to my stomach. As much as I disliked Ryan – and God, did I dislike him now – I knew that wasn't true. But in a bid to trip him up, Mr Kinch started mentioning other girls Ryan had been with and that one of them had admitted sleeping with Whant too. While they were speaking about this girl, Ryan admitted that there had been some 'overlap' between her and Nikitta, several years ago when Nikitta was around sixteen. I remembered how she'd sat in the house and moped around, waiting for him to get in touch as her friends went out and enjoyed themselves and I wanted to scream. Who did he think he was? Some sort of player? I know he was only a kid but I was still driven mad with rage. If Nikitta had just dumped Ryan as she should have done way back then, none of this would have happened.

But, of course, she hadn't dumped him, so we had to keep listening.

'I suggest you and Nikitta had sex while Whant was in

the flat,' Mr Kinch said. 'I suggest you called Mr Whant in and said he could have sex with Nikitta while you ironed your shirt.'

'No, that's not true,' Ryan said.

I know Mr Kinch had a job to do but I wanted to punch him. How dare he talk about my daughter in such a disrespectful way? But what was about to follow really made my head spin. Mr Kinch was suggesting that Ryan had been trying it on with one of the girls in the flat in Corelli Street. Her name was Elizabeth Taylor. We'd been told she was giving evidence the next week because she was Ryan's alibi.

'The fact is, you were hoping something would happen between you but you are not prepared to admit it,' Mr Kinch said. I could tell Whant was loving this, as he kept scribbling things down on the piece of paper he had in front of him. Occasionally, he would look at me, just to see how all this was going down with me. It was sick.

Again, Ryan said, 'That's not true.'

Soon, Mr Kinch ran out of questions and Ryan was free to go. By now I was in turmoil; I didn't know what to think. Had Ryan been trying it on with this other girl, or was Mr Kinch just trying to trip him up? He'd also suggested Nikitta had agreed to have sex with Whant and that was beyond ridiculous. But could this be true? I just didn't know what to believe.

As Ryan took his seat in the public gallery, next to his mum, just along from Paul and me, I felt my cheeks burn with anger and confusion. I couldn't look at him so I stared straight ahead.

In the end, I decided it couldn't be true. It just couldn't. Taking cocaine and staying out all night was one thing but betraying my heavily pregnant daughter quite another. In his own way Ryan had doted on Nikitta and I just couldn't let myself believe he'd done this. I couldn't bear to think how much it would have broken Nikitta's heart.

What was done was done. Ryan was no more able to turn the clock back than I was and I had to convince myself that he bitterly regretted not going home earlier that evening.

The case was adjourned for the weekend and, of course, we had the first anniversary of Nikitta's death to deal with. When I'd seen Kerry's name flashing up on my phone a year previously, I'd never imagined what she was about to say would change my life forever. But it had, and now I had to deal with it. It was a bitterly cold day and we took some yellow roses to the graveyard. We always made sure the pots next to Nikitta's headstone were full of flowers but it was so cold that the old flowers were frozen solid and the water in the pots had turned to ice. Paul had to chip away at the pot so we could swap the flowers round.

We were all wrapped up and it had started to snow. My fingers were numb inside my gloves and the snowflakes stung my face. For a moment, the court case didn't matter; I wasn't even pissed off at Ryan anymore. I just wanted to hold Nikitta and Kelsey-May in my arms – to reach into the ground and somehow pull them back to earth.

'This is a terrible thing to say,' I began. 'But I wish someone would hurt him the way he has hurt us.'

Paul pulled me into a hug without saying anything. For a

few moments we stayed by the headstone, crying softly but not saying a word. We were both still crying as we got back into the car and the snowflakes fell on the windscreen.

The harsh weather didn't let up for our return to court the next day. Elizabeth Taylor was the first witness. Ryan was sitting a few seats away from me and I had decided to try to be civil but for some reason Whant was looking at me even more than usual. It made my skin crawl.

Elizabeth Taylor started speaking about how she and her friend had gone back to Corelli Street to take cocaine with Ryan, Daniel and Whant. Of course, I'd heard all this on the Friday but it didn't make it any easier to swallow. When Mr Taylor had finished with her, Mr Kinch began his cross-examination.

'Would it be right,' he said, 'to say that Ryan Mayes was paying particular attention to you? He seemed quite interested in you?'

Elizabeth Taylor shook her head before saying, 'It was nothing more than flirting.' I couldn't help but notice that she looked like a little girl. She must have been a year or two younger than Nikitta. What the hell was she doing hanging around with them, taking cocaine?

'Ryan Mayes didn't tell you he had a partner, did he?' Mr Kinch continued. I could feel the blood pumping round my body and rushing to my head, the sweat forming on my palms and the panic rising in my throat. 'As far as you knew, he was unattached?'

Elizabeth Taylor nodded slowly. Her eyes swept the room, as if she was looking for Ryan in the public gallery. She looked a little unsure of herself. She must have been an adult, or she'd have had to give her evidence from behind a screen but to me, she was just a silly little kid who'd got mixed up with a bunch of no-hopers.

Mr Kinch paused for effect before delivering his next question. 'There was a bit of...' – he glanced at his notes, as if looking for the right word – 'snogging, wasn't there?'

Paul put his hand on my arm as I sucked my cheeks in. My heart was racing and I could hear it thumping in my chest as I waited for the stranger in the dock to speak. I was sure it was so loud that everyone in the court could hear it too. I didn't dare look at Ryan; I was scared of what I would do if I did.

Elizabeth Taylor looked at the ground, then met Mr Kinch's eye. 'I just kissed him,' she said with a shrug. 'That's all.'

At this point, Whant spun round to look at me. He had that weird look on his face again and his eyes were like lasers, slowly seeping into me and burning my soul. I felt like my world was collapsing for a second time as I tried to process what I'd just heard.

Nikitta had died because her boyfriend was locked in a strange bedroom, kissing someone else.

I'd never warmed to Ryan but I thought of all that Paul had done for him over the past year. He'd taken him in, looked after him and poured him drinks as they'd laughed and cried over Nikitta. And all the time, Ryan had known what he'd done. He'd known he'd betrayed our daughter just days before she was due to give birth to their first child. He'd gone to that party in the early hours, knowing she could have given birth at any second, and he'd chosen to stay and chat up someone else.

It all made perfect sense, now. Whant was so cunning. We'd heard from other witnesses that he'd spent most of the night downstairs, chatting to girls on Facebook while Ryan and Daniel flirted with the girls they'd met in the club. He'd been desperate to have sex but he was fast running out of options. The girls at the party weren't interested and he was being ignored by most of the people he tried to contact online. His girlfriend would be in a mood because he hadn't come home like he'd promised. But Ryan also had a girlfriend at home – a beautiful girlfriend who would be all alone because he was busy trying his luck with someone else. Whant had always wanted to sleep with Nikitta. Now he knew for a fact that she would be home alone, heavily pregnant and vulnerable, with no one to protect her.

I could just see the grin spreading across his sick, smug face as everything slotted into place and the plan formed in his head.

My head was spinning so much as I looked at Whant in the dock that I didn't realise Mr Kinch was still talking. He was asking Elizabeth Taylor if Ryan had tried to go any further – if he'd wanted more than just a kiss – but I couldn't bear to hear her answer. A few seconds later court was adjourned for a short break. As Whant was led away in handcuffs, he stared right at us. I know he wanted to see me jump from my seat, grab Ryan and scream and scream and scream – and God, that was exactly what I wanted to do. Like a pressure cooker of emotion, I was going to explode – it was only a matter of time. But as Whant's disgusting, goggly eyes swept over me, I did something I never thought I was capable of: I held his gaze with my steely stare and then I reached over and grabbed Ryan's hand in mine. Whant looked so confused and, for a moment, I felt the faintest bit of satisfaction. I had to act like I already knew about this, like it wasn't a shock. I had to pretend we'd known about it for ages so he couldn't get the big reaction he'd been hoping for. If I could keep my cool now, I could keep my cool any time – at least in front of him. He couldn't bring me down.

Needless to say, as soon as he was out of my sight, I dropped Ryan's hand like it was a hot potato. I didn't even look at him as I ran from the court, Paul following behind me. None of our family so much as looked at Ryan as they followed us outside. As I tore through the front door and out into the biting wintry air I was too angry to cry. I lit up a cigarette and took a drag, waiting to feel some kind of release, but nothing changed; I was still ready to swing for Ryan. I hoped he wasn't stupid enough to follow us outside but within seconds, he was hot on our heels, like a little lost puppy.

'I'm sorry,' he said, kicking his heels, his eyes on the ground. Now the fury that had been bubbling inside me was ready to spill over.

'Sorry?' I spat. 'You're fucking sorry, Ryan? *Sorry?*'

'Yeah,' he said. 'I'm sorry.'

'I actually cannot believe we are having this conversation,' I thundered. 'You left my pregnant daughter home alone to take drugs and snog another girl? She was nine months pregnant, Ryan. Do you remember that? Nine months pregnant with your bloody baby! Did you care about that? *Did* you? Did you even give a shit about Nikitta? Because it certainly doesn't seem like it!'

Paul was standing beside me. He stubbed out his own cigarette. 'You are out of order,' he said. 'It's not just the cheating, it's the lying. Do you have any idea how that felt for us, sitting in court hearing that without a word of warning?'

Ryan said nothing.

Paul went on, 'You can't say you didn't have the chance to tell us because you did. You have come round to our house almost every night. We've taken you in and treated you like one of our own because we knew Nikitta would have wanted us to look after you. How the fuck could you do this to us? Don't you think we've been through enough?'

'I just didn't want to upset you,' he said, kicking the gravel beneath his feet. 'It was just a kiss and a bit of flirting; it was nothing to worry about. It didn't mean anything.'

'It didn't mean anything!' I shrieked, incredulous. 'It didn't mean anything! I'm sure it would have meant something to Nikitta if she'd found out. How do you think that would have made her feel, knowing you did this when she was nine months pregnant, about to give birth to your baby? Would she have thought it was nothing to worry about? *Would* she?'

'I... well... I,' Ryan stuttered, but I wouldn't let him finish.

'Tell me, Ryan! Tell me! Would she have thought it was nothing to worry about?'

His face twisted uncomfortably and I wanted to punch him. 'I just didn't want to wreck the relationship with you,' he said.

'Well, Ryan,' I said. 'I will tell you now what will wreck your relationship with me – making me sit in a courtroom, face-to-face with the man who killed my daughter, and listening to how he had the perfect opportunity to do so because you – yes, Ryan, *you* – were too busy getting coked up to your fucking eyeballs and chasing anyone who would look at you. Don't you have any bloody shame?'

'I'm sorry,' he said, again. 'I really am. I didn't want this to happen, I loved Nikitta.'

'Well,' I said. 'So did I. More than you will ever know. And I will never forgive you for this, as long as I live.'

Paul put his arm around me. 'Come on, Ryan,' he said. His tone was far more reasonable than mine but I didn't know how he'd managed not to grab Ryan and smack him. 'All we were ever told was that you'd gone out to watch the rugby. There's a bit more to it, isn't there?'

'I guess so,' Ryan said.

I looked at my watch and, realising it was time to go back into court, I stubbed out my cigarette.

'Ryan,' I said, 'I will be civil to you until this case is over but only because getting justice for my daughter and my granddaughter is far more important than you will ever be. I do not want your fucking twat of a cousin to see how angry I am at you because he will love every minute of watching me fall apart. So, the minute we get back in there, I will not shout at you. I will not even raise my voice. I may even comfort you and hold your hand.' I fixed my eyes on him but still he would not meet my gaze. 'Look at me, Ryan.'

He lifted his head and, squinting a little, he looked me in the eye.

'When this is over,' I said, 'we're done.'

Chapter Seventeen

Whant in the Dock

I know it might sound silly but I spent the next few days wondering how I'd break the news of Ryan's infidelity to Nikitta. I couldn't bear to write in my diary because I couldn't stand to mention it. I tried to imagine what I'd do if she were still alive and I'd caught him cheating just before Kelsey-May's birth. She'd have been absolutely heartbroken. How could I ever have found the words to comfort her?

I was still struggling to accept that she was gone and I wanted to be as tactful and understanding as if she was still alive. It just didn't feel right writing in my diary and speaking about the case without mentioning it, as it was all our family and friends could talk about. Most of them were giving Ryan the cold shoulder. Some of the guys even wanted to hit him but Paul and I told everyone in no uncertain terms that they were not to touch him. We were better than that and we'd rather he was punished by thinking about what he had done.

Eventually, three days after Elizabeth Taylor had given her evidence, I took out my little blue book and started to write:

Sweetheart, Ryan hasn't been completely honest with us. I don't want to write and tell you what he's done because I think, wherever you are, you already know somehow. He has had ample opportunity and he has never said a word. Silly boy, Keet! I hate him for it, I absolutely hate him. I know that you would probably forgive him, Keet, if you were here with us, but you're not, so what now? He should have been home with you, in your arms! It guts me. I can't help but think of what you are feeling now! There are a million and one things running through my head but I can't even bear to put them down on paper. Stupid, stupid boy! I feel for him but I will never, ever forgive him and I will never, ever forget – unless I know you want and need me to.

A few days later we were told that Whant would be taking the stand in his own defence. When Ian broke the news to us, a horrible chill shot down my spine. I'd hoped his solicitor would decide not to let him give evidence in case he incriminated himself. I couldn't bear to hear the lies he'd tell about Nikitta.

I knew he was desperate to see what his lies were doing to us and to Ryan. Every time I caught a glimpse of Ryan sitting a few seats away from us in court, my stomach tightened and I felt sick. Quite frankly, he disgusted me and I wished I didn't have to look at him but we had to put on a show of unity or Whant would get his sick wish. It was really, really hard.

When Whant emerged from the dock, he was wearing a black suit, a striped shirt and a black tie. He looked ridiculous because everyone was used to seeing him wandering around Broadmead Park in a scruffy tracksuit. Again, he fixed his eyes on me – or that's certainly how it felt.

Mr Kinch cleared his throat before asking his first question: 'Did you rape and stab Nikitta Grender?'

It was so cut-throat, so brutal, so straight to the point. I knew he was a lawyer with a job to do but it never got easier, hearing those awful words in the same sentence as Nikitta's name.

'No,' said Whant, with that horrible glint in his eye. 'Never.'

Paul held my hand in his as Mr Kinch began to question him further and he started talking about how he and Ryan liked to take drugs together. The blood started to rush to my face.

'Nikitta was all right,' he added. 'Though I heard through other people she wasn't keen on me.'

But what happened next made me want to jump up and scream. Mr Kinch started questioning him about when he'd apparently had a kiss and a cuddle with Nikitta, several years beforehand.

'I was drinking at a friend's house and I contacted her,' he said. 'I was just bored; it was something to do. She was staying at her parents' house. We arranged to meet. We talked for ten or fifteen minutes then it started to rain. We had a hug and kiss and then she left. More could have happened, possibly, but it wasn't my intention.'

I had to keep looking straight ahead and staring him in the face but I wanted to scratch his eyes out. He was speaking about my daughter as if she was a piece of meat – some silly little girl he could call up, then just cast off – when everyone knew how much he fancied her.

'You OK?' Paul whispered.

'Yes,' I said, without taking my eyes off Whant. 'Yes, fine.'

Nothing could have prepared me for what followed. Mr Kinch started to ask Whant about the day before Nikitta had died. At first it was pretty formulaic. He spoke about how he and Ryan had been working, canvassing for a double-glazing firm, and how they had then returned to Newport to watch the rugby. They'd called at Broadmead Park so Ryan could change his clothes. Up until that point, his account was consistent with Ryan's.

A few days earlier, Ian had explained to us about the vaginal swabs – about how Whant's semen had been found inside Nikitta. He told us that was how the police had been able to charge him with rape. Ian warned us that Whant would probably try to claim the sex with Nikitta had been consensual, in a bid to look like he was innocent. That in itself was sickening but, even in my wildest dreams, I couldn't imagine the cover story he'd concoct.

I had to catch my breath as he began to tell the jury how, while they'd been in the flat, Ryan had gone into the bedroom he shared with Nikitta. After around ten minutes, Whant claimed Ryan had called on him. He said he'd opened the door to find Nikitta and Ryan having sex.

'He asked me if I wanted to have a go,' he said. 'To have sex.'

Whant had stammered through most of his evidence but he said this sentence as clear as a bell and with his eyes fixed straight on me. Next to me, Paul put his head in his hands and I could see he was choking back tears. I felt like someone was slowly twisting a knife into the pit of my stomach. Nothing could be more horrifying – more downright degrading – than this. How could he stand there and claim our beautiful daughter had agreed to have a threesome with him and Ryan at any time, never mind when she was just about to give birth? It was so ridiculous and even though I knew in my heart of hearts that the jury would never believe him, it still made me sick to my stomach to hear him say it.

'It was just one of those things,' said Whant with a shrug, as if he was talking about some run-of-the-mill everyday task. 'It just happened. I don't think I said yeah or OK, or anything. When I finished, Ryan was in the kitchen ironing his jeans. Afterwards, I just got dressed and went into the kitchen. It was unexpected. I don't know why it happened.'

For a few moments, I regretted ever wishing he'd plead not guilty because I was sure I couldn't take another second of his pathetic lies. Why on earth did I ever think I'd have the strength to sit through a trial? For the first time since the pathologist had begun to describe Nikitta's injuries, I knew I had to have a break. Some of our friends and family had already fled the court in tears. Shakily, I got up and slowly walked out of the public gallery. I knew Whant was looking at me, so I kept my composure but as soon as I got out, I felt the tears stinging my eyes and spilling down my face. Paul wasn't far behind me and he took me in his arms and stroked my hair for a few seconds. As he placed his head on my shoulder, I realised he was crying too. It was so, *so* hard.

'After everything he's done,' said Paul through his sobs, 'after everything, he has to go and say this; to talk about Nikitta like she was a piece of meat.'

I hated seeing Paul so upset, as he always tried to hold it together for my sake. Now that he was in tears, I felt like I had to find some strength from somewhere.

'Let's go back,' I said after a few minutes. 'We need to do this for Nikitta.'

Paul didn't say anything but he locked his fingers in mine and slowly we shuffled back to our seats. Whant was still on the witness stand, grinning as if he was down the pub, telling his mates about a great night out he'd had. To him it was all one big joke – how could he be so cruel?

But he was still spinning his ridiculous story and enjoying every minute of his lies. He was even describing the underwear Nikitta had been wearing and that made me want to vomit. Paul's face was contorted with pain and anger. I gave his hand a squeeze.

Mr Kinch asked Whant why he hadn't mentioned having sex with Nikitta in any of his previous police interviews.

'I thought it was a stupid thing to have done,' he said and shrugged. 'I felt bad because I had a fiancée. I didn't want to cause any embarrassment for anyone – Ryan, my girlfriend or me. I didn't think it through. It wasn't a sensible thing to do.'

Then Mr Kinch started questioning him about the scratch marks on his arms. This was really, really hard for us, as we couldn't bear to think about Nikitta trying to fight him off. Although he claimed they were from the fight in the pub with the Asian man – a fight we seriously doubt ever happened – we knew how he had got them and it killed us.

I tried to focus but my mind kept wandering to that awful night. I'd been sleeping peacefully as Paul and his friend Lloyd had their nightcap downstairs, all oblivious to Nikitta's terror. Of course, there's no way we could have known. What parent expects their child to be brutally murdered in their own bed by someone they know? Before it happened to us, I could never have comprehended such a thing.

But still I couldn't help but think, what if? What if she'd just phoned us? Her phone was always beside her bed – it was rarely out of her hand. What if she'd just managed to reach out and grab it and dial my number? My phone was next to the bed anyway because I'd urged her to call me if she thought she was going into labour. I'd have woken with a start and heard her screams and I would have run round to the flat just as fast as I had the next morning when Kerry phoned to tell us about the fire. By this point, Paul would have been downstairs and I'd have grabbed him on my way out. Even though he'd have been a bit worse for wear, he'd have sobered up in an instant when he realised how serious it was.

'Nikitta's in trouble,' I would have said. 'We've got to go now.'

He'd have dropped the drink he was holding and he'd have sprung to his feet. The glass might have shattered into a thousand pieces but we would neither have seen nor heard it because there would have been only one thing on our minds: saving Nikitta.

Just like we did on the following morning, we'd have got there within minutes – maybe even seconds. But this time, there would have been no fire engines outside, no one telling us we couldn't get to her. Paul would have battered the door down, screaming like a madman, and, eventually, he'd have managed to get in. I'd have been close behind him – probably on the phone to the police, breathless and panicked, urging them to get there as soon as they could.

Just in the nick of time, we'd have heard the sound of sirens and as Paul ran up the stairs, taking them two at a time, police officers would have been hot on his heels. They'd have grabbed Whant from Nikitta and wrestled him to the floor. She would have been in an absolute state, of course, and I'd have held her close to me, comforting her as he was led away in handcuffs, but amid the revulsion I would have had another overpowering feeling: relief.

Relief, because my girl still would have been here.

'OK, Marce?' Paul asked hoarsely and I snapped out of my trance.

'Yeah,' I whispered, with a weak nod.

As I zoned back in, Mr Kinch was asking Whant about the journey he'd taken in the early hours of the morning Nikitta died. He was lying through his teeth again, still claiming he'd gone to get cigarettes from his grandmother but that he'd gone a less direct route because he was scared of being pulled over by the police as he'd been drinking and taking drugs.

It had all turned out so differently. He'd climbed into his car, drunk, high and crazed with lust for my gorgeous girl. And he'd armed himself with a knife, as he knew there would be no other way he'd ever get to have sex with her.

She hadn't managed to get to her phone, so we'd stayed at home, Paul drinking while I slept, with no idea of the horror she was facing. There were only two people who knew what really happened that night: Whant and Nikitta. Nikitta was gone and Whant would never tell the truth, so we had to accept we'd never really know for sure what her last moments were like.

All we could guess is that he'd been too strong for her. If she'd cried for help, no one had heard and now, there we were, with nothing to do but sit in a cold courtroom listening to the gruesome details of how she'd died as we watched her killer try and wriggle out of it.

Thankfully, Mr Taylor, however, was razor-sharp in his cross-examination.

'These events happened in February last year, your statements to police were in February last year, and interviews were in February last year,' he told Whant. The barrister then looked at the jury, pausing for effect before he continued. 'It wasn't until December of last year, Mr Whant, [that] the prosecution received notice from you [that] your case had changed. Is there any reason why it took so long?'

'It was in my head going round and round, and I decided to just tell the truth,' said Whant.

'When you tell the jury you had sex with Nikitta Grender, it's made up,' Mr Taylor retorted. 'It's pure invention, isn't it?'

Whant shook his head but Mr Taylor wasn't finished.

'You need to say something to explain the semen, don't you?' he went on.

Whant glared at him. 'You can think what you want but that's what happened,' he said.

Then a statement was read out to the jury. It was from one of Whant's first police interviews, in the days following Nikitta's death.

As Mr Taylor read the words aloud, I felt my throat tighten. 'Nikitta was the first person I thought of when I fancied sex,' he said, looking Whant in the eye.

For the first time, Whant looked a bit uncomfortable, as if it was suddenly starting to dawn on him that his game might be up; that he might not get away with this after all. How stupid he had been thinking that lighting one silly match would outwit dozens of detectives and lawyers.

'That's been confused,' he glowered but we all knew there was no way such a disgusting statement could be misinterpreted.

'OK,' Mr Taylor said. 'You were giving the police the impression Rachel is your life. You don't actually care much about her, do you?'

'That's totally wrong,' he replied.

We all knew this was yet another lie. Whant had made a

promise to go back to his fiancée and have a night in with her, yet he'd blown her off to drink and take drugs and rape and murder a young woman and her unborn child in cold blood. It sent a shiver down my spine. I didn't know his girlfriend but I did wonder how she'd be feeling now. Night after night she'd slept next to this monster, with no idea what he was capable of. I thought of the little boy who had bounced on Nikitta's lap when she'd brought him round to our house and I had to catch my breath as I realised this girl had given birth to his children. What must she be thinking now?

It wasn't long before 4pm arrived and it was time to go home. The journey back to Broadmead Park was a daze.

'We all know he's guilty,' Mum said to me as I unlocked the back door and dropped my handbag on the kitchen floor. 'The jury will see through his lies.'

'They will, Marce,' Paul's brother Mike agreed. 'No one in their right mind would believe a word that came out of his mouth.'

Leaving the door open, I lit up a cigarette and inhaled deeply.

'I know,' I said and sighed, the smoke circling in a cloud around my face. 'I just can't bear the thought of them even considering he might be innocent.'

'It won't happen,' said Paul. He'd stepped outside to smoke too. 'We have to keep thinking that. It won't happen.'

I just wanted to go to bed and hide for a few days but I knew that wasn't an option so, as always, I turned to my diary:

I was livid and horrified that he took the stand but a liar always gets caught out. I think – and so does everyone else – that the jury will see him for what he is: a cold, callous, calculating, sick, lying bastard. It was hard today, Keet – so bloody hard. Your dad got upset a couple of times. That kills me but I think it makes me stronger. It kills me because I have to see the person I love, who loves his daughter so much, break down and cry and then I've got to sit in the same room as the twat who has ruined everything and hurt the man I love.

But I have to be strong. Still, I'm not sure if I can listen to any more and I imagine you can't either, sweetheart. They need to let you all rest now – you need to. Love you, sweethearts, I'm missing you like crazy! I wish you were all here to hug. Goodnight, sweethearts xxx

When we returned to court the next day, the defence continued its case but they didn't have half as many witnesses as the prosecution because their case was based almost completely on Whant's warped and false version of events. As I looked at Mr Kinch and the team of lawyers he'd enlisted to help him, I did feel a little curious. I knew they had a job to do and I understood the fact that that everyone is entitled to a lawyer, no matter what they are supposed to have done. After all, we were constantly reminded that, in the interests of justice, Whant had to get a fair trial. Paul and I had tried so hard to abide by the rules to make sure this was possible and that he didn't get off on a technicality.

I couldn't help but wonder, though, if Mr Kinch had a

daughter himself. How would he feel if he'd got Whant off? Would he really be happy, or would it have worried him that a predatory, violent sex offender was still walking the streets, free to do to someone else what he had done to Nikitta? Would he lie in bed and worry about this, or would he simply tell himself it was all part of the job? But I didn't have much more time to think about it because soon it was time for Mr Taylor to sum up for the prosecution. After clearing his throat, he faced the jury and he didn't mince his words.

'Someone went into that flat and committed those crimes,' he said gravely. 'And we say that someone was Carl Whant. I'm not being sarcastic but how very unfortunate for him that the only time he had consenting sex with Nikitta Grender was about twelve hours before she was murdered.'

His tone was withering as he turned to look at Whant in the glass dock. 'I submit that Carl Whant will say anything if he thinks it helps him,' he continued. 'We know from Ryan Mayes and from Nikitta's mother, Marcia Grender, that she did not like Carl Whant. I submit that Nikitta Grender was raped by Carl Whant and she punctured his skin with her nails, trying to fight him off.

'How very unlucky that, on the night when Nikitta Grender is to be raped and murdered, he has this run-in with an Asian man. How very unlucky to receive those injuries when Nikitta Grender was killed in this way.' He was still looking at Whant. 'It is obvious, we say, that Nikitta Grender caused these injuries herself, trying to fight him off.

'He never went to his Nan's house to get cigarettes. This is another embellishment. And how did Nikitta's blood get on the inside of his jacket and his shirt?'

Some of the jury members were scribbling notes on the paper they'd been given. Mr Taylor paused for a second.

'Then we have the blood in the car,' he continued. 'A car Nikitta had never been in.'

It was then the turn of Mr Kinch.

'What help it might have been if someone around Broadmead Park was having a sleepless night and was able to tell us what was going on,' he said. I wanted to scream. If someone had been having a sleepless night, Nikitta could have been saved. Mr Kinch went on, 'We have to face up to the fact there is no direct evidence from machine or person. All we have is circumstantial evidence. It's the same as putting a jigsaw together. Some pieces fit and some pieces don't.'

He took a deep breath and paused, as he surveyed the jury.

'It follows, as night follows day, that whoever set the fire killed Nikitta Grender. Are we all sure Carl Whant is proved guilty? There's no shame in the answer: we just don't know.'

It was so pathetic that I almost laughed. If that was the best he could come up with, I had no idea how the jury could acquit Whant but the thought was still lingering at the back of my mind, silently torturing me.

In the end, his speech was so rambling and dull that one of the reporters who had been covering the case fell asleep on the press benches.

But the last word went to the judge, Mr Justice John Griffith Williams.

'Nikitta Grender was a pretty young woman who was

happily facing the imminent prospect of motherhood,' he told the jury. 'Understandably, the circumstances of her death shocked and upset a number of people and attracted a great amount of media attention at the time and since. There was and is a considerable amount of sympathy towards Nikitta's family. You must put out of your mind feelings of sympathy and prejudice for and against anyone in this case.'

And with that, he sent them out to consider their verdict.

Chapter Eighteen
The Verdict

The jury was sent out on Tuesday, 21 February 2012 and the significance wasn't lost on us: it was the same date as Kelsey-May had been due. Had this nightmare not happened and had she come on schedule, we would have been celebrating her first birthday. It was so surreal.

If things had been different, we'd have been arranging her birthday party. There would have been pink balloons and lots of cakes and Kelsey-May would no doubt have been dressed in a beautiful party dress. She'd have been spoilt, of course. I would probably have been buying her presents for months, as much as Paul would have scolded me. Yet here we were, stuck in this nightmare parallel universe, which had become our lives.

We had decided to wait in the canteen for the verdict. Paul and I could have had a private room but there were so many of our family and friends with us that we would never have all fitted in. Plus, it was more convenient to sit near the doors, as we could then pop out for a much-needed cigarette.

Luke had come along to court for the sentencing. Paul and I would never have let him sit through the trial and hear all the horrendous details of how his sister had died but we wanted to give him the chance to hear the verdict.

He'd come along to court but he'd spent most of the day nervously staring at the floor.

'Mum,' he said, 'would you mind if I maybe didn't come in?'

I instinctively wrapped my arms around him. 'Of course not,' I said. 'One of your cousins will wait outside with you.'

Luke didn't raise his head. 'I feel like I'm letting you down,' he replied.

'Luke, of course you're not letting me down,' I said. 'It's your choice.'

'I want to be here,' he said. 'I just don't want to be in the court.'

I was so angry that Luke had to go through any of this. He was only fourteen and he should have been hanging out with his mates without a care in the world.

In the end, the jury only had a few hours to deliberate, so they were sent away, to return the next day. Thinking of the sleepless night ahead was agonising, but in a way, I was glad the jury hadn't come to a conclusion. It would have been such a bittersweet way to mark what should have been Kelsey-May's first birthday.

Paul and I tossed and turned all night. By now we'd slotted

into a little routine of hanging out of the window, smoking, waiting for sunrise and wondering what fresh horrors the new day would bring. Now it was nearly over but it was a strange feeling. I was sure Whant would be found guilty – I just couldn't let myself think of the alternative. But, as much as we wanted him behind bars, it wouldn't bring Nikitta, Kelsey-May or Missy back. Our lives would go on, still with the huge gaping void, and we'd just have to find a way to adjust.

Morning eventually came and Ian drove us to court as usual. He told us that, if there was a guilty verdict, the press would be desperate to speak to us and suggested it might be better to have a prepared statement we could read from the court steps, rather than risk being seized by reporters as we made our way out.

'I'll help you write it,' he said. 'And maybe you could read it, Paul?'

Paul looked at me with panic etched on his face. We both knew he'd never be able to do it. The trial had been such a huge ordeal and he didn't like public speaking under normal circumstances.

'Can I ask my brother to do it?' he said.

'Of course,' Ian replied. 'Whatever you think is best.'

We knew that only Mike would have the strength to stand up and speak for us, just as he had done at Nikitta's funeral. He really was a tower of strength.

Minutes felt like hours as we sat in the canteen, waiting for the jury to reach a conclusion. Dazed, I couldn't really hear or see what was going on around me. All I could focus on was the verdict. I knew there was enough evidence to convict Whant – there just had to be. How could the jury find him not guilty? It just couldn't happen.

After what seemed like days – but in reality had been just a few hours – Ian told us it was time to go back into court.

'The jury has reached its verdict,' he said softly.

Luke had come to court again but this time he'd decided to stay in the canteen and have a hot chocolate with his cousin Shaniece instead of coming into the public gallery with us, as he'd explained he wanted to. I just wanted to grab him and hold him but I knew I had to go back into court.

Paul grabbed my hand. Both of our palms were sweaty and my stomach was somersaulting.

'He's guilty,' said Paul. 'He has to be, Marce. He has to be.'

The courtroom was busier than we'd ever seen it before. Even though cameras weren't allowed in court, there were reporters everywhere, some of whom had followed the trial every day and others we'd never seen before. The public gallery was packed too. Although we'd had around thirty family and friends come along to the trial every day, now there were around seventy of us. Many people couldn't afford to take weeks on end off work but they had wanted to come and hear the verdict.

One by one, the jury members took their seats. It felt strange knowing our fate – or rather the fate of the monster who had killed our daughter – was in their hands. For a month now I'd sat and looked at them almost every day and they knew so much about my family and what we'd been through, yet we didn't know a thing about any of them. I couldn't help but wonder how the weight of responsibility in such a horrific case had affected them.

We were told by an usher to stand as the judge entered the courtroom. By now we had got used to the strange court rituals and they were almost second nature to us.

The judge started by warning us there had to be no disturbance while the verdicts were being delivered, although he understood it was a very emotional time for us. Paul and I had already warned everyone to try their best to contain their emotions until we got out of court. The last thing we wanted was to give Whant the satisfaction of causing a huge drama.

The courtroom fell silent for a few seconds before the judge spoke again. He asked the foreman of the jury to stand and deliver the verdicts they had reached on each charge. Paul squeezed my hand so tightly that I could barely feel it and I could taste the blood in my mouth as I bit the side of my cheek.

'In relation to charge one on the indictment – the rape of Nikitta Grender – how do you find the defendant?'

The foreman looked straight ahead as he said, 'Guilty.'

'And in relation to charge two on the indictment – the murder of Nikitta Grender – how do you find the defendant?'

There was a pregnant pause. You could have heard a pin drop in the courtroom as we all waited for his answer.

'Guilty,' he said.

I could hear a few sobs ringing out around me but I didn't take any notice because all I could think about was poor little Kelsey-May.

'And in relation to charge three – the charge relating to child destruction – how do you find the defendant?'

'Guilty,' came the reply for the third time. I exhaled deeply as the foreman confirmed the jury had found Whant guilty of arson too.

My eyes fixed on him as the last of the verdicts was announced. I wondered if he'd be shocked. After all, he'd seemed so sure he would get away with it.

But he didn't react at all. In fact, he yawned. Can you believe it? He just yawned, like he was bored of hearing about our daughter and granddaughter and how they'd lost their lives. Like it was old news.

I can't describe how I felt. All I know was that I remained stony-faced and I looked completely emotionless. If only people knew how many private tears I had shed! Many people have asked if I felt relieved in that moment and I suppose I did, in a way. It was reassuring that Whant would be locked up; that he'd have to pay for what he had done. But no verdict would ever bring the girls back. It was hardly a time to jump up and down and celebrate.

A few seats away from me, Ryan was sitting with his head in his hands, sobbing. Paul gave him a little pat on the shoulder but I didn't know quite what to do. For a moment, my steely facade slipped and I reached out to hold his hand. I still couldn't forgive him but for our own sanity we needed to put on a united front.

I wasn't sure if the judge would want to take stock before sentencing Whant but everything seemed to pass in a blur and before we knew it, Mr Kinch was reading Whant's previous convictions to the court. He'd never been convicted for violence or sexual assault before. No one had had any idea what he was capable of.

'You have expressed no remorse and in an act of quite extraordinary hypocrisy, you even took flowers to the grieving Grender household,' Mr Justice John Griffith Williams told Whant. 'You are a calculating, vain and devious individual and the explanation for this terrible crime lies, in part, in your vanity.'

There were still a few people sobbing around me but I felt frozen, rooted to the spot.

'You fancied Nikitta and you wanted to have sex with her,' he went on. 'You knew she was unlikely to agree to consensual sex, so you went armed with a knife to rape her. The likelihood is that she let you in, thinking that Ryan was with you.

'You were able to overpower her but not before she put up some resistance and scratched you. She probably made it clear she was going to report you to police for rape and that's why you killed her.

'You destroyed the life of Nikitta's baby, who would otherwise have been born alive and, by setting fire to her bed, you destroyed large parts of her body so her family and Ryan Mayes could not see her face for one last time.'

I tried not to think about the police mortuary and how I'd had to touch Nikitta through a velvet cloth; of how Whant had deprived me of the chance to kiss my beautiful girl and look at her lovely face one last time.

'You left her family, Ryan Mayes and her friends

bereft,' the judge continued. 'The subsequent loss was compounded by the knowledge that her murderer had raped her and then tried to destroy her body. The grief was made all the more deep because you did not scruple to make the wholly false allegation that she had consensual sex with you.'

He looked at Whant, who still seemed completely indifferent, wearing the same bored expression as he sat impassively in the dock.

Finally, the judge said, 'I sentence you to life imprisonment, to serve a minimum of thirty-five years.'

All I could think of as we descended the steps from the public gallery was Luke. I just had to get to him. Nothing else mattered. I wasn't sure where anyone else was – I didn't even know where Paul was. I took the steps two at a time as I ran outside, my heart thudding in my chest.

I heard his voice before I saw him. He was outside the courtroom with Shaniece, asking frantically where we were. He looked so little and so vulnerable and, for a moment, it felt like he was just a little boy again. I ran to him and, as he caught sight of me, he began to run too. Like most teenage boys, he was usually fairly reserved with his emotions but today was totally different. He launched himself at me and threw his arms around my waist.

'Is it a guilty?' he said. 'Mum? It is, isn't it? It's a guilty!'

I couldn't speak so I just nodded. Luke broke down in my arms, sobbing like a baby. It was only then that my own tears came too. I could feel Paul wrap his arms around my shoulder, like he had appeared out of nowhere. For the next few moments, we just held each other and wept.

Eventually, Ian gently ushered us out onto the court steps. He'd already warned us the press would be waiting and they were out in force. I could hear the clicking of the cameras as the cold wintry air stung my face.

Paul's brother Mike made his way to the front of the crowd, clasping the piece of paper on which we'd drafted our statement. He was to speak second, after David Wooler, the Crown Advocate for the Crown Prosecution Service in Wales.

'When we reviewed the initial evidence against Carl Whant gathered by Heddlu Gwent Police back in February last year, the truly horrific nature of the crimes committed was all too apparent,' Mr Wooler said. 'At that stage, it was clearly appropriate to authorise a murder charge in relation to Nikitta Grender's death. However, the offence of murder cannot be committed against unborn children and we felt it was extremely important that Kelsey-May's death was marked by a separate charge in its own right.'

Paul put his arm around me and I was aware that I was staring at the ground. I didn't want to look up yet and see the flashing lights of the cameras – I just didn't feel like I could face it.

'Carl Whant was, therefore, also charged with the offence of child destruction, under the Infant Life Preservation Act 1929,' Mr Wooler continued. 'This piece of legislation – thankfully, very rarely used – can help protect the rights of an unborn child that is capable of being born alive. Kelsey-

May undoubtedly fit that description. This is an offence which prohibits wilful acts causing the death of any child capable of being born alive and, given the advanced stage of Nikitta Grender's pregnancy, Kelsey-May certainly fit that description.

'Child destruction is, thankfully, a very rarely used charge. We are not aware of another case like this one in Wales. When the legislation was originally drafted in the 1920s, it was intended to be used to curb the activities of backstreet abortionists. But in a more modern setting, it can be applied to cases where an offender deliberately takes the life of an unborn child through a violent or aggressive act.

'As the police inquiry continued over the weeks and months following the original incident, more evidence became available to us, ultimately leading to the addition of rape and arson charges against Carl Whant.

'I think many of us involved in highly emotive cases such as this one experience a strange mixture of emotions at its conclusion. Whilst we may feel that a conviction provides vindication for the immense amount of hard work that goes into a major criminal investigation and prosecution, we are acutely aware that today's verdict does not bring back Nikitta or Kelsey-May.

'Equally, whilst we may move on to our next case, the family and friends of the victims are left to grieve their loss for many years to come. All we can do is hope that today's conviction at least allows them to take one small step forward in rebuilding their lives. A large number of people have supported this trial as witnesses and we would like to thank each and every one of them for their strength and resilience.'

I was suddenly aware of DCS Ronayne standing in front of me. It was like he had appeared out of nowhere too but suddenly he was giving a statement too.

'We are satisfied that justice has been served today with the conviction of Carl Whant for the horrific murder of Nikitta and Kelsey-May,' he said. 'Whant has never admitted his guilt, given any indication as to why he committed this terrible crime or provided Nikitta's family with any answers. Gwent Police officers worked tirelessly and thoroughly with colleagues in the Crown Prosecution Service to present comprehensive evidence to the court to ensure the best opportunity for conviction.

'We also sought advice from experts from across the UK in various disciplines to strengthen the case against Whant. We have endeavoured to do our utmost to get justice for Nikitta and Kelsey-May. We have also done our best to provide support to Nikitta's family, and our thoughts, as they have always been, are with them today. With the murder of Nikitta and Kelsey-May, they have lost their daughter, sister and granddaughter, and Ryan has lost his girlfriend and daughter.

'The family, and Ryan, must be commended for their bravery and dignity and for the support they have given to the police investigation over the last twelve months. This process has undoubtedly been a harrowing ordeal for them. I'm hopeful that this conviction brings to an end one part of that process, although, without a doubt, they will continue to mourn and grieve for Nikitta and Kelsey-May for the rest of their lives. Also of note is the support we, as an investigative team, have received from the community of Broadmead Park and Moorland Park and we are confident that they will continue to support the family throughout this difficult time.'

I finally found the strength to raise my head as Mike cleared his throat and began to speak. He was the last person who would address the press.

'My name is Michael Brunnock,' he said. 'I am the brother of Paul Brunnock and I am Nikitta's uncle. On behalf of Paul, Marcia, Luke, Ryan and the immediate family of Nikitta and Kelsey-May and the larger family circle, we would like to thank Gwent Police for the investigation and the support that we have received over the last twelve months. We would also like to thank the prosecution team which has represented us.

'The last twelve months have been harder for us than you can ever imagine and, as a family, we remain in total disbelief about what has happened. Nikitta was so young and beautiful and she and Ryan were set to become a very proud set of parents to Kelsey-May. This has been ripped from them by Carl Whant, who has never had the decency to tell us the truth.'

Mike took a deep breath. Paul put his arm around me as I squeezed Luke's hand.

'For us to see our grandchild for the first time in a mortuary was the most heartbreaking thing we've ever had to do,' Mike went on. 'Nikitta was so special and will remain in our hearts until we die. We will never deal with the tragic events that have stolen our family from us but we hope we can, at least, start to understand what has happened. Thank you very much.'

DCS Ronayne gently ushered us towards the waiting police car.

'Best get inside,' he said, 'or the press will start to hound you now.'

I slid into the car and closed my eyes for a second. I still hoped, when I opened them, I'd realise this had all been a terrible dream.

Chapter Nineteen

A New Life

On the evening of the verdict, we went to a pub in the centre of Newport. To call it a celebration would be wholly inappropriate. Nikitta, Kelsey-May and Missy were gone forever. There was nothing to celebrate. I suppose it would be more fitting to say that we wanted to mark the occasion.

One long, hellish month was at an end and we had the result we wanted – of sorts. Whant was in jail, which was the best we could have hoped for under the circumstances. We were overwhelmed by the number of strangers who nodded respectfully as we walked past, or gave us a gentle pat on the back.

I suppose I had to put in an appearance at the pub but it was the last place I wanted to be. I've said before that I've never found any comfort in drinking. It was a strange anticlimax. We were relieved we'd no longer have to listen to Whant's lies or any of the awful details of how Nikitta had died, but what now? The weeks would turn into months and the months would turn into years and she'd never, ever be coming back. How were we supposed to get over it?

The answer was that we wouldn't get over it. We'd just have to learn to live a new life; a new life in which we tried to manage the pain. It would be a bit like having a chronic illness. Some days we'd have a flare-up and we wouldn't be able to leave the house because the pain would be so great. Other days we'd just about get by. We'd paint on a smile and face the outside world, as bravely as we could, but no one would know how much we were suffering inside.

I knew I would never be the same person I was before the fire. Part of me had died with Nikitta and Kelsey-May and there was no point in trying to pretend otherwise. Sometimes I'd drag myself out but a lot of the time I didn't feel like socialising. Most people were lovely to me but they just didn't know what to say and it made me feel awkward.

One morning, shortly after the trial, I popped to the post office to run some errands. There were two older ladies standing outside, chattering away. I wasn't even listening to their conversation until I heard them mention the word 'murder'.

'Did you hear about it?' the first lady said, her permed grey hair shimmering in the spring sunshine. 'That girl down on Broadmead Park? The guy got thirty-five years.'

'Not enough, if you ask me,' said her friend. 'I hear she was eight months pregnant.'

I pushed past them and into the shop, my heart beating

nineteen to the dozen. They hadn't recognised me, of course, and they hadn't meant any harm but it was still horrible and it almost put me off going out. Everyone seemed to be talking about Nikitta and there were reminders of her everywhere I turned. I could only hope that, in time, the hype would die down.

What hurt the most, though, was the number of people who crossed the street to avoid me – often people I had known for a very long time. One afternoon, I was shopping at the retail park across from our house when I stopped to take some money from a cash machine. Out of the corner of my eye, I spotted an old friend – one of the girls I'd hung around with in Ringland all those years ago when I'd first got with Paul.

I saw her before she saw me. For a second I took my eyes off her to collect my money and put it in my purse when I heard her little boy asking her if he could go and have a look in one of the sports shops.

'No,' she said. 'I've been in every bloody shop now! We're going home.'

I looked up and I was all set to go over and speak to her. She was zipping up her little boy's jacket and I could tell she had seen me out of the corner of her eye. I expected her to turn round and come over to chat, maybe even give me a hug. It had been a while since we'd hung around together but we had been really close as teenagers before life and kids got in the way. Still, we always had a nice chat when we saw each other in the street.

Today, though, she turned on her heels and sprinted into

the nearest shop before I could say a word. She didn't even acknowledge me. I was left standing in the middle of the car park, clutching my purse, feeling hurt and confused. Then it dawned on me: I hadn't seen her since Nikitta had died. It was clearly all a bit too awkward for her.

I suppose a tragedy like ours helps you understand who is really there for you. Paul and I were blessed to have such a supportive group of family and friends around us and for that we were thankful. They have never deserted us but we have always been conscious of the fact that they have their own lives to lead. Gradually, for the sake of everyone's sanity, things had to return to some kind of version of normality.

For us, though, life was to turn into a series of never-ending battles. The first was our bid to have Nikitta's flat razed to the ground. I heard through the grapevine that four separate families had moved out of the neighbouring houses after the fire. Some of them didn't even know Nikitta but they just couldn't deal with the idea of bringing up their children in full view of such an awful crime scene. I didn't blame them. Although we had returned to the flat a few times to gather some belongings, I tended to avoid walking past if I could help it. It made it all the worse that it looked just as it had the day Nikitta had died, the smashed windows giving a full view of the burnt-out rooms inside.

We spoke to the council first of all and they said they would look into it. I was stunned when I received a phone call to say the downstairs tenant wasn't willing to move out and that they couldn't demolish the flat until she agreed to vacate the property.

This made my blood boil. The downstairs tenant was, of course, Sarah Voisey. She'd come to court to give evidence, she'd seen us all sitting ashen-faced in the public gallery and yet she was happy to continue living in the building where our daughter had been raped and stabbed to death. I was so angry that I decided to go round there – I don't know what I hoped to achieve but I had to have it out with her. I suppose I'd always resented her a bit for not raising the alarm earlier when the smoke detector started to go off, even though we'd never know for sure how serious she thought it was.

It was a gorgeous summer's day when I went to see her and she was outside in her garden, chatting to a neighbour I knew a little. I exchanged a few pleasantries with the neighbour before I turned to Sarah.

'I'm sorry to interrupt,' I said, 'but can I just ask: are you comfortable living here? You know, given what's happened?'

'Oh, no,' she said, breezily. 'That doesn't bother me, that.'

I shook my head in disbelief. 'Well, I'm sorry, but don't you think that's a bit sick?' I asked. 'Don't you know the council wants to take this whole building down?'

'Ha!' she said. 'I ain't moving out for that, no way! They've got a fat chance of getting me out.' As she looked me up and down she paused for a second. 'Who are you, anyway?'

I couldn't believe how downright ignorant she was. I pursed my lips as I said, 'I'm Nikitta's mum.'

Suddenly, her expression changed and she gasped and practically ran into the house.

'I'm not talking to you!' she cried behind her, without turning round. 'I'm phoning the police.'

Now I was gobsmacked. I hadn't done anything wrong – I'd just asked her to explain what I thought was a very strange decision. I was even more baffled, though, when I got a knock on the door a few hours later from a couple of police officers, who wanted to know if I'd been harassing her. For a few seconds I was struck dumb. My daughter was dead and yet she was playing the victim? Of course, they didn't take any further action but Paul was so mad that he went round there and asked her to explain herself.

'I just don't want to move,' she said. 'I've been here for ages. I like it. Why should I go?'

'But the council is going to get you a new place,' he said. 'You won't be out on the streets.'

'I just don't want to move,' she replied. 'I'm fine where I am.'

I suppose, technically, she was within her rights but how anyone could live in such a place I have no idea. The thought of it is enough to give me nightmares.

In time, Paul and I started to go back to working full-time. I had been working on and off for a bit, but there were long stretches when I just couldn't face it. However, in the end, it was good for me to have some sort of a routine. Paul struggled a bit more because his job involves driving for miles alone. He had too much time to think and it took him a while to readjust. Eventually, he just had to get on with it. We needed the money so we had to work; there was just no two ways about it.

I dreaded the long school holidays, though – days and days of nothingness, which should have been filled with

Kelsey-May's laughter and Missy's barks, as I cooked dinner for Nikitta and gave her some advice about motherhood. I'd spend entire days sitting by her headstone, crying quietly and talking to her like she was right there. After a few months, I stopped writing in my diary. In the first few months it had been my salvation and throughout the trial, but the more I wrote, the darker my thoughts became. In the end I decided that it was doing my fragile mental state more harm than good.

One summer afternoon, after I'd spent an entire day sitting on the grass next to the headstone, I was feeling particularly fragile. Paul came to pick me up. As we were driving home, we hit a traffic jam in the centre of town. My heart nearly stopped as we pulled up beside a van and saw Whant's dad in the driver's seat. He was sitting with his feet on the dashboard, singing along to his radio as if he hadn't a care in the world.

'Look at him!' I said to Paul. 'Is that who I think it is?'

'It is, Marce,' said Paul. 'But just leave it. He's not worth it.'

'But I've just finished breaking my heart crying and he's sitting there whistling, like he's having the time of his life!' I cried. 'How can he just go on like nothing has happened?'

'Marce, leave it,' Paul told me. 'Just sit here, don't say anything. He isn't worth it.'

But I was on a mission – I couldn't help myself. The window of his van was down, so I rapped on the door and he turned round to look at me. I don't think he realised who I was at first but then I could see it slowly dawning on him.

'I cannot believe you can just sit there and whistle along to your radio like nothing has happened!' I shrieked. 'Do you know what your son has done to my family? Have you any idea?'

I couldn't help myself then. The venom was spilling from my mouth but he just sat there, calm as anything.

He said, 'My son is innocent in all of this.'

I was incredulous. 'Innocent?' I echoed. '*Innocent*? Are you blind? Are you stupid? *Innocent*?'

Paul had come out of the car now and laid his hand on my shoulder.

'Your son is a murderer and a rapist!' he shouted to Whant's dad. 'Why can't you see that? He's been locked up for thirty-five years! Come on, Marce. Let's go.'

It was only then that I realised how deathly quiet the street had become. People had rolled down their windows and switched off their car radios. There were even some shopkeepers standing out on the pavements, watching us. My cheeks burned scarlet as I got back into the car. It made me mad that people were getting some sort of sick entertainment from my distress but I didn't regret what I'd said.

As for Ryan, needless to say, he started to drift away pretty soon after the trial ended. I couldn't stand the sight of him and now I made no effort to disguise it. Paul was a little more charitable and invited him round occasionally, just to see how he was getting on.

'I see a bit of myself in him, Marce,' he said. 'He's done some stupid things but he's just a daft kid.'

To be completely fair, I think Ryan did appreciate what

Paul had done for him – he certainly said that he did. But just a few weeks later, I heard a rumour going round that he had got with a schoolfriend of Nikitta's. I tried to ignore it because I just didn't want to know but it knocked me for six when I heard she was pregnant. I had to find out the truth, so I confronted him one day when I saw him at Nikitta's grave.

'Don't take me for a fool, Ryan,' I said, 'because I will find out.'

He insisted the girl wasn't pregnant – I think he even denied that she was his girlfriend, but of course she was. A few months later, I received a text from Kerry saying she was now the proud grandmother of twins – a boy and a girl. I'd always thought Kerry was OK, but I was so upset that I deleted her number. I was supposed to be a grandmother too and it felt like she was rubbing my face in it, even if she hadn't meant any harm.

Paul, as ever, was more reasonable.

'He's got to get on with his life, I suppose,' he said. 'But it just hurts that he had two babies with her friend.'

'It should have been us,' I said, sobbing. 'It should have been us and Kelsey-May. It's just so unfair.'

Perhaps in his own strange little way Ryan did want to build bridges because he asked Paul if he could bring the twins round to visit us.

'No, Ryan,' said Paul. 'We don't want to see your babies. No disrespect but we don't. I think it's time we drew a line under this, once and for all. You get on with your life and we'll get on with ours.'

Epilogue

I still don't know if my Nan did see my future on that warm summer's day all those years ago, but if she did, in a way I'm glad she took it to her grave with her. I'm glad I was allowed to live for thirty-seven years of my life without this burden, which now weighs me down every single day – a burden that I will take with me to my own grave.

I still have that horrible gnawing feeling in the pit of my stomach. It's with me from the minute I wake up until I fall asleep at night. Every morning I wake up and I have to deal with the reality that Nikitta – not to mention Kelsey-May and Missy – are not here and they're never coming back.

There are so many things I miss about Nikitta. I miss feeling her soft skin as she hugged me, I miss singing my songs to her, I miss teasing her about how vain she was – I even miss worrying about her and telling her off. I'd give anything to have her back, even if it meant going mad at her for being so stubborn, or forking out for yet another McDonald's as she said the words she knew would get her pretty much anything she wanted: 'You knows you loves me.'

For me the worst time of day is teatime, around 4.30pm, when I get in from work. The house is so quiet that I could cry. Missy isn't scratching at the door, yelping to get inside, desperate for her tray of chicken.

On Saturdays I buy a little less bacon and not so many eggs as there is one less fry-up to cook. On Sundays often I can't face making a big roast, especially if it's lamb because I know that was Nikitta's favourite.

Life is boring now – *really* boring. We should have had a house full of love and laughter but, instead, it's deathly quiet. Luke is an adult now and he's moved in with a friend. He still comes back to visit regularly but I really feel the pain of having an empty nest. No one can ever fill the void that has been left and it would be foolish to pretend they could.

On good days, I can focus on little positives. While the murder of a child often drives supposedly unbreakable couples apart, my relationship with Paul has survived. In fact, I'd say it's stronger than it has ever been before. We don't sweat the small stuff now. Things we'd have argued about before seem insignificant. As long as we have food on the table and a roof over our heads, nothing else matters. It's just not worth stressing about.

We still have Luke and even though he is a man now, we have to look out for him and look after him. You never stop worrying about your children, no matter what age they happen to be. I wonder what things would have been like if Nikitta had been an only child and I had no one else to focus on – no one else to live for; no little part of me anywhere else. It doesn't bear thinking about.

Most days at work I can manage to find Miss Grender. In a way, it has been my salvation. Sometimes I even go into school in the holidays to help make displays and prepare work because it's better than sitting in my empty house thinking of what should have been.

At home, though, I'm still Marcia. I'm still broken and no one will ever truly be able to put me back together. The pain of losing my three girls will be with me to my dying day but I can only hope they know we loved them, as Nikitta always said.

We loved them, and we always will.

Acknowledgements

My family and I would like to thank everyone who helped make this lasting tribute to Nikitta a reality: our agent Clare Hulton and our editors, Chris Mitchell and Anna Marx.

On a personal level, we would like to take this opportunity to express our gratitude to the countless people who helped us through the most traumatic time of our lives, and who are still there for us today. Our list is endless. If you are not named, it does not mean we are not deeply grateful to you for all you have done for us.

Firstly, we want to thank our parents for being there for us when we needed them the most. You are still living this nightmare with us, yet you have always helped us deal with our pain as best you could. Thank you from the bottom of our hearts. We are also so grateful to our siblings and their partners, especially Michael and Elaine. You were unbelievable, Mike. You are our strength, our voice and our rock and we thank you so much.

We'd also like to thank our large extended families: our aunts, uncles and cousins. In particular, my Uncle Paul and Auntie Tracey, who were there for me every day: if you weren't with us in person, you were on the phone constantly. You took us places to occupy our minds and you replaced all of the kettles we went through, making endless cups of tea and coffee for our visitors. You also made sure our cupboards were always full when feeding ourselves was the last thing on our minds. You were, and still are, amazing. This is why I have always said you are like my second parents. Thank you both so, so much.

Patrick and Cheryl: you were there any time of the day and night and you looked after Luke for months on end. You were his rock and you kept him safe and sane. You have shared so much with him and with us. Thank you both so much.

To our friends: there are so many of you that we couldn't mention you all by name but there are a few people we have to thank individually.

Donna and Griff, you are two very special people. Thank you for all of the events you organised in Nikitta's memory and for all the things you are still doing for us. You are both amazing and so thoughtful. We are so lucky to have you as very dear friends.

Lloyd, thank you for taking Luke under your wing. You are like the brother he never had and you have always helped keep him occupied. You were there on the morning we received that awful phone call. I'm so, so sorry to you for that – but you have been Paul's rock. Thank you for being there for him when he needed you and being such a good friend to all of us.

We'd also like to thank Nikitta's friends. I know it was – and still is – very hard for you all, but you keep her memory alive. Thank you for visiting her, Kelsey-May and Missy. I know she appreciates and loves it as much as Paul and I do. Please keep telling all of the stories you have about her.

We are also grateful to everyone who played a part in Nikitta's short life, no matter how big or small. To all of the teaching staff and the agencies who helped her get into work – all of you sent condolences, cards, flowers or messages. Thank you for all of your kind words and for sharing your memories of Nikitta at various stages in her life. It means a lot to us that you all took the time to get in contact with us.

I would also like to thank everyone at my place of work, Ringland Primary School: governors, staff and parents. Thank you for the patience, understanding and support you gave me. You will never know how you touched me. Lisa, my headteacher – you were, and still are, like my counsellor. Caroline, you are such a good friend – you make me laugh, and you make me cry. Above all, you know me. Thank you both and every other member of staff so much.

To everyone on our estate, and to all of the companies who sent us lovely messages: you helped restore some of our faith in mankind.

Jane and Dave – wow, you are amazing! Two complete

strangers who stepped into our lives and made things a lot easier for us. What can I say? You make me cry whenever I think of you – I never thought that people like you existed. You are unique! My tears are falling thick and fast right now, trying to think of something to say to you both and I am simply lost for words. Nothing I can say will ever be enough to thank you for what you have done. I know Nikitta would have loved to have met you and she'll be watching over you, thanking and helping you in any way she can. Your family are so lucky to have you in their lives and so are we. You are always in our prayers and thoughts. Thank you from the bottom of our hearts.

To Ian, Ginny, Paul and everyone at Gwent Police, who did such a great job of bringing Carl Whant to justice and ensuring he will not be free to hurt another innocent person for a very long time, if ever. What would we have done without you? You are worth your weight in gold. You kept us occupied with all of the tasks you set us. You saw us crumble and helped us back up again. Ian, especially, you kept us focused. We can't thank you enough. We would also like to say a huge thanks to Geoff Ronayne for leading the investigation in such a professional manner and for giving up so much of his own time to make sure the police involvement in our story was accurately represented in this book.

We'd also like to thank everyone else who helped ensure justice was done in Nikitta's name: our barrister, Greg Taylor; the judge, Mr Justice John Griffith Williams, and, of course, the jury who saw through Carl Whant's lies.

God bless every single one of you.

ACKNOWLEDGEMENTS

With all our love,
Marcia, Paul, Luke, Nikitta, Kelsey-May and Missy Moo
xxx